Marilyn Manson

THE UNAUTHORIZED BIOGRAPHY

Copyright © 2007 Omnibus Press
(A Division of Book Sales Limited)

Written by Doug Small
Cover designed by Sarah Nesenjuk
Book designed by EMA

ISBN-10: 0.8256.7347.X
ISBN-13: 978.0.8256.7347.4
Order No. OP52239

Exclusic distributors:
Music Sales Corporation
257 Park Avenue South
New York, NY 10010, U.S.A.

Photo Credits:

Every effort has been made to trace the copyright
holders of the photographs in this book but one or
two were unreachable. We would be grateful if the
photographers concerned would contact us.

Steve Jennings/WireImage.com: 1, 78, 91, 96b; Lili
Wilde/All Action/Retna: 6, 7, 29, 31, 56, 57;
Rodolphe Baras/LFI: 3, 18, 49, 51, 67, 77; Joe
Hughes/LFI: 4, 5, 27; Redferns/ Retna: 8, 10, 15, 20,
21, 36, 46; Gary Malerba /Corbis: 11, 16, 44, 45; M.
Gerber/Corbis: 13; Kristin Callahan/LFI: 22; Frank
Forcino /LFI: 25, 32, 74, 79; Justin Thomas/All
Action/Retna: 26, 55, 61; Ilpo Musto/LFI: 30;
Milkman: 33; Suzanne Moore/All Action/ Retna: 39,
54; Sin/Tony Mott/Corbis: 40, 58; Kelly A.
Swift/Retna: 42, 43, 48, 68; Stills/ Retna: 52, 53, 5
Kevin Mazur/LFI: 65; Sam Hain/LFI: 66; Dana
Frank/Corbis: 69; John Galdwin/All Action/Retna:
70, 71; Kevin Mazur Archive/WireImage.com: 75, 8
84, 105b, 111, 112; Kevin Winter/Getty: 83; Scott
Gries/Getty: 87; John Shearer/WireImage.com: 90,
108; Barry King/ WireImage.com: 92; Frank Mullen/
WireImage.com: 95; Diena/ Brengola/ WireImage.com:
96t; Christina Radish: 97; Tim Mosenfelder /Corbis:
98; Jeff Vespa/ WireImage.com: 99; Scott Barbour/
Getty: 100; Jemal Coutess/Wireimages.com: 103;
Stephane Cardinale/ Corbis: 105l; Jesse Grant/
Wireimage.com: 105t; Rune Hellestad/ Corbis: 106

Front Cover Photo: Nicolas Guerin/Corbis
Back Cover Photo: Tim Mosenfelder/Corbis

Printed in the United States of America by
Vicks Lithograph & Printing Corp.

WHAT in GOD'S NAME is GOING ON?

The full-frontal assault that is Marilyn Manson took the Nineties music scene by the throat, garnering chart success and critical acclaim while simultaneously whipping the moral majority into such a frenzy they were late to church. Fast-forward to 2007 and Manson hasn't loosened his grip, with his latest in an impressive string of hit albums—*Eat Me, Drink Me*—set to sustain his stranglehold.

Ever since *Antichrist Superstar* hit the unsuspecting U.S. charts with a Number Three debut back in 1996, Manson has been waging a full-on war against conservative groups whose hysterical cries of outrage against the rock star they've mistaken for Satan have ensured that barely a date on world tour after world tour has gone by without protest, controversy, or cancellation.

Their frontman, Manson, namedrops to the tune of Nietzsche, Darwin, and Milton in conversation and says things like "the juxtaposition of diametrically opposed archetypes" when asked what Marilyn Manson means. Hey, he might not be the best looking guy on iTunes, but he may well rank among the most intelligent. As *New York* magazine put it, "For a guy with a woman's name who likes to perform in a G-string and hernia truss, singer Manson gets a tremendous amount of respect." He may scare the hell out of some people, but his core ethic is actually pretty right-on: This "dirty, dirty rock star" advocates freedom of expression and the importance of art and individualism. The uproar persists, but Manson has proven himself to be a provocateur who can be relied upon to create ever-evolving and enduring art.

From the swamplands of Southern Florida they came, a whacked out little outfit called Marilyn Manson and the Spooky Kids. Feeding themselves on nursery rhymes and magic tricks, they grew and grew until they were big enough to leave the death-metal scene of their youth and head to the candyland of MTV and record deals. Their fearless leader had hatched a fiendish plot, and the beautiful people weren't watching their backs...

PRELUDES and PREMONITIONS

Once upon a time, in a land called Ohio, the future "antichrist superstar" was born and christened Brian Warner. His childhood was, by all accounts, as normal as the next. So when did little Brian begin his metamorphosis into Marilyn Manson? Is it possible to trace his medical accessories fetish to Manson's mother's nursing career or to the numerous times her rather sickly son was hospitalized with pneumonia? Can his tending-toward-obsessive fondness for self-mutilation and disfigurement and his disjointed, crippled stage movements be attributed to the times he and his Vietnam Vet father spent in government tests and meetings regarding the effects of Agent Orange? These events undoubtedly played a part in forming the Marilyn Manson of today. The articulate rock star whose main philosophy is one of individuality also admits to having enjoyed an upbringing he has often cited as being supportive of his unconventional ways.

His early days seem to have been a fair mix of dark and light. Manson's recollections run the gamut of Willie Wonka–influenced happiness to hints of trouble and trauma. He has been oft quoted as remarking that abuse comes in many forms, not all of which are physical. "My father had a very violent temper, and he was never home. So I was kind of a mama's boy," Manson disclosed to *Rolling Stone* in its January 23, 1997, cover story on the band. He went on to confess, "I wish I could go back and change the way I treated my mom because I used to be really rude to her." Furniture salesman Hugh Warner's present-day role seems to be bursting-with-pride father. Warner Senior, who has been known to attend quite a number of Marilyn Manson gigs, announced to *Alternative Press* in its February 6, 1997 issue that, "I knew he was going to be great, whatever he did. He's very dedicated, he does 100 percent. And I'm very proud of him - he's the 'God of Fuck.'" An odd

mixture of the comments section of a teacher's pet's report card, the recollections of childhood neighbors of the President, and a token bit of Manson-inspired profanity—but the words of an apparently loving 'rent nonetheless. Manson's father was also quoted in *Rolling Stone*'s June 26, 1997, issue as stating that his son "wants parents to raise their children right, and that's probably what's wrong with our society today. They don't always give children the freedom or respect they deserve."

The lead singer's first encounter with the stage was all but encouraging although oddly appropriate. Playing the part of Jesus in a school play, the little six-year-old future Marilyn Manson sported only a towel as his son-of-God costume ("I wasn't wearing any underwear because I didn't know any better," he explained to *Q* magazine). The towel was duly ripped off the young Manson's skinny frame, and he was suitably traumatized in front of the entire school. Hmm, such an early account of Christianity-tinged sexual humiliation could explain a few things.

Of the good old days in the private Christian school in which his parents enrolled him, Manson recalled to *Q* magazine in July 1997, "I was ostracized there and did my hardest to misbehave and get kicked out. During prayer when everybody had their heads bowed I used to steal money out of the girl's purses. There was one time I put a vibrator in my bible teacher's desk." One doubts whether that childish prank was greeted with a "kids will be kids" shrug—we must assume that the future Reverend Manson wasn't caught red-handed on that occasion. "I used to do a lot of things that, now that I look back on them, were kind of amusing," he reminisced to *Metal Edge* magazine in August 1997. "I would set up myself as a candy dealer, like your modern-day drug dealers, because the kids weren't allowed to have gum in Christian school, and I would peddle it to them at overcharged prices."

When, how, and why the ringleader-to-be began to question the value of authority and convention and to form his own burgeoning view of a different kind of society is impossible to pinpoint. One thing is for certain; Brian Warner would most definitely fulfill the wish he would later howl in song: "I wanna grow up/I wanna be/a big rock and roll star."

the CHOCOLATE FACTORY

The first meeting between the creators of a band that would terrorize the right wing of the United States is, alas, undocumented. However, it is known that Manson, sick and tired of his stint as a music journalist, met up with like-minded Daisy Berkowitz, and the two decided to create a mad mixture of music, theater, and mayhem together; hence Marilyn Manson and the Spooky Kids was established in 1989. The name Marilyn Manson "was a pseudonym I had taken on because it kind of defined my style, what I was saying," Manson explained to *Guitar World* in December 1996, adding, "And phonetically, the way it flows, it almost sounds like 'abracadabra.' It has real power to it." One of the musical venture's concepts was the idea behind combining the opposites and celebrating the extremes of life and in doing so pushing it all to the limit. Years later Manson rationalized to *Circus* magazine in its June 17, 1997, issue, "Light and darkness, life and death are simply two inseparable parts of life. . . . Good and evil go hand in hand." And what better way to illustrate this point than by joining two all-American icons, Marilyn Monroe and Charles Manson? Daisy Duke of TV's *The Dukes of Hazzard* and "Son of Sam" murderer David Berkowitz provided the inspiration for Daisy Berkowitz's new title, and the first two Spooky Kids were ready to hit the streets for the trick-or-treat campaign of the century.

The band's earliest incarnation was allegedly the four-man, one-drum machine ensemble that featured Manson and Berkowitz along with bassist Olivia Newton Bundy (Aussie songstress Olivia Newton John and Ted Bundy—put to death in Florida that very year) and Zsa Zsa Speck (the one and only Zsa Zsa Gabor and nurse-murderer Richard Speck). The official line-up took form before the start of 1990 however, with two new, more permanent members who were quite happy to adopt the surname of a murderer and the first name of a female icon, and hence Gidget Gein took over on bass while Madonna Wayne Gacy took his stance behind the keyboards. The Gidget and Madonna monikers surely need no explanation; Ed Gein was a cannibal and John Wayne Gacy the killer of thirty-three young boys.

Marilyn Manson and the Spooky Kids put on quite a show right from the start. Squeeze—a small Fort Lauderdale, Florida, club—was host to many of the band's early gigs, some of which have since become legendary due to word-of-mouth, hype and exaggeration, and even bootlegged videos—filmed by the band's first camcorder-clutching fans—since copied and circulated in trading circles. Jack Kearney, Squeeze's owner (who gets a mention in the "thanks" section of the band's first album), recounted to *Rolling Stone* in its June 26, 1997, issue that at one 1990 gig Manson "had a girl named Terry tied to the cross and semi-naked" and added that, in true telephone-game style, before the night was over the incident had been exaggerated to the point that "[people] were saying she was totally naked and her throat was cut." Of course, the bandmembers—and bandleader—have become more and more outrageous, visually and idealistically, as Marilyn Manson's career has progressed, and such initial Florida gigs in tiny clubs did not, needless to say, present the band in its present-day finery due to the lack of space, high-tech gear, and money to spend on sound, lights, and special effects. However, the core of what makes a Marilyn Manson live show unique was most certainly in evidence at these early shows. Mr. Manson himself, sans tattoos and sporting the eyebrows he was born with, may not have immediately appeared as otherworldly and frightening as he does on stage today, but on closer inspection back then it was not difficult to see the dirty rock star about to emerge. His now-familiar battle with the mic-stand was already in full form, and his manic pounding of it against his own chest and shoulders caused the naked little Barbie-type dolls tied to its wires to perform their own accompanying dance.

The alternately articulate interviewee and animal-like performer we all know and love was plain to see right from the start. The incongruence of the future Reverend's howling, driving vocals with his incredibly calm and mild directions to the stage crew (the likes of "Turn down the mic and the monitors, please," or "Hey mister soundman, can you turn up the drums?" were so persuasively delivered that the desired effect was almost immediate) did not seem to phase his early fans who embraced his schizophrenic leanings as one of his unique charms. Already delivering "inspirational"—if a little unclear—speeches (excerpt from the November 1989 Squeeze gig: "What does a man know about his children, you know?" and "What I hear from you people is you come up to me and you say, 'Save the rainforest, save humanity.'. . . What you gotta do is save yourselves."), Manson was no run-of-the-mill death metal dude.

Nor did his band blend into the background. Daisy took to turning up for gigs in pretty little numbers complete with women's wigs. Madonna, affectionately known as Pogo after his murderer's nickname (Wayne Gacy, when not on a killing spree, moonlighted as a clown for children's parties), set up shop on stage with a "Pogo's Playground" tent.

Manson's present-day predilection for on-stage destruction is nothing new; at one early gig at the aforementioned Squeeze he pulled out (amongst other things better left unmentioned) a chain-saw, sawed through some of the set, and apparently put the fear of God into the young

woman housed in a cage at the back of the stage. Other antics at this particular show included Manson making what appeared to be a peanut-butter and banana sandwich and tossing it into the cramped crowd and a seemingly simulated sex act between Manson and the caged girl during the crowd favorite "Cake and Sodomy." Of his violent tendencies while performing, Manson would in August 1997 confess to *Metal Edge* magazine that "it's part of the adrenaline of being on stage, there's a real fearlessness and a sense of numbness and immortality, so often I don't know my own strength and my own limits."

A typical Spooky Kids show back then featured "stage sets" chock-a-block with nasty little toys and devilish decorative touches. Sharing the tiny stage with the band on any given night might be a large shaved doll's head on a stake, a Lite-Brite set spelling out the charming message "Anal Fun," an enormous hat festooned with banners and flowers, an American flag, or a music stand from which Manson might pause momentarily to read aloud from Dr. Seuss's *The Cat in the Hat*. Bloodied and dirty children's clothing was festively hung from a clothesline with care. All of this was but a teensy taste of what was to come.

ABRACADABRA

At the time, however, it seems that a little madcap kick-up-the-ass was just what the doctor ordered for the Florida death-metal scene. In the midst of a revolving roster of misery merchants, another black-haired, tattooed Satanist with a scary voice and a dislike of sunlight was unlikely to cause heads to turn. It was the Marilyn Manson entertainment ethic that stood out from the crowd. And the band didn't stop at creatively conjuring up outrageous stage antics and props. They began building a little empire, a sort of Spooky Kids Experience that took it upon itself to pop up here, there, and everywhere. By performing live on local radio and publishing and distributing their own flyers featuring artwork by Manson himself they further promoted the concept of Marilyn Manson so that the band took on a larger identity. Fans could even take a little spookiness home after the show - the group may not have had a commercial release, but why let that stop them? They produced their own "promotional" cassettes and sold them at gigs. Those very same cassettes, limited in number even then, have now taken on enormous collector's value as well as near-mythical status. Whispers of the existence of the earliest cassettes, entitled *Big Black Bus* (in honor of the original Manson family's mode of transportation), *The Meat Beat Cleaver Set, Grist-O-Line*, and *Snuffy's VCR* can be heard at any meeting of self-respecting Manson fans. The band continued this tradition well into 1993 with the more officially documented *After School Special, Lunchbox, The Family Jams*, and *Refrigerator* tapes. Although there are these days duplicate copies in circulation, the rare originals—design and artwork courtesy of Manson and Berkowitz—are treasured by precious few.

The earliest documented Manson flyer heralded the inauguration of the fifth member of the Spooky Kids and the band's first human drummer. The now-immortalized "Marilyn Manson & the Spooky Kids: The Family Trip to Mortville" brochure announced the arrival of new family member Sarah Lee Lucas, duly credited with "baked goods, percussion." Such a wholesome namesake had yet to be chosen, and the coffee-cake-plying Sarah Lee was

paired with the heinous Henry Lee Lucas without further ado. The Mortville flyer featured staple sketch subjects—from the pen of Marilyn Manson himself—lunchboxes, guns, and needles. Perhaps suitably threatening imagery for Sarah Lee, whose days with the band were numbered.

With a live drummer backing the band, the Spooky Kids' own brand of lunatic's special music began to form up quite nicely, thank you. Crowd favorites "Cake and Sodomy" (with its ever-popular "I am the god of fuck" Charles Manson quote), "My Monkey," and even strangely twisted covers of ditties like Black Sabbath's "Iron Man" were hummed on the way home, as it were, and even taught to kids as bedtime lullabies. You may scoff, but the nursery-rhyme cadence of "My Monkey" ("I had a little monkey / I sent him to the country and I fed him on gingerbread / Along came a choo-choo, knocked my monkey coo-coo / And now my monkey's dead") caught the fancy of a fan's son, and six-year-old Robert Pierce not only sang on the track when it was recorded for the band's first album, but also made a guest appearance in the "Lunchbox" video.

The Spooky Kids carried on terrorizing and tantalizing the humid, mosquito-filled swamplands of Southern Florida with their outrageously entertaining freak show. Amidst all of the asylum-style showmanship and maniacal backstage partying, the band was becoming a tighter and better outfit musically, and their notoriety was growing and growing. The Florida metal music scene did not kowtow to middle of the road, run of the mill, sissies-only kudos like the Grammies, and had as the ultimate tribute its own Slammy Awards ceremony. In 1992, Marilyn Manson and company took home two skull-shaped trophies for Band of the Year and Best Hard Alternative Band. Notably, another winner that year was one Jeordie White, who claimed the Best Rhythm Guitarist Slammy for his riffs with black metal band Amboog-A-Lard. As White, now known as Twiggy Ramirez, was to tell *Rolling Stone* in its January 23, 1997, issue, "The day I met him [Manson], I knew we

would work together. As the band gained popularity local-
ly, I thought it was my place to either be in the band or
destroy it." After Marilyn Manson (the band had shed its
Spooky Kids skin for a more stream-lined image, and its
lead singer had become simply Mr. Manson) had garnered
two more Slammies in 1993—Band of the Year yet again
and Song of the Year for "Dope Hat"—Twiggy Ramirez
opted, in true "if you can't beat 'em, join 'em" style, to sign
on. By December of 1993, he had officially become the
bassist for Marilyn Manson, replacing Gidget whose drug
addiction is often blamed for his departure from the band.
Of his name, Twiggy would later tell *Guitar World* in
December 1996, "I like Richard Ramirez because he was
into heavy metal music. And I chose Twiggy because she
was androgynous. She liked to dress up like a little boy."

Manson's first meeting with his true right-hand man
allegedly took place in that all-American institution, the
shopping mall. Mr. Manson—perhaps on a reconnaissance
mission of sorts—bumped into the future Twiggy, and the
pair began mischief-making post haste. The gruesome
twosome's maiden deviant joint venture was to torment an
unsuspecting young female shopkeeper with death-
threats and prank calls from a payphone a few feet away
from their prey. Their efforts soon expanded beyond such
fairly run-of-the-mill adolescent antics, and they jump-
started two musical projects together. Twiggy (mas-
querading as a woman) was the lead singer in Mrs.
Scabtree, with Manson on drums. More interesting, however, is their other undertaking, the bogus Christian metal
group Satan on Fire, whose inspired single was entitled
"Mosh for Jesus."

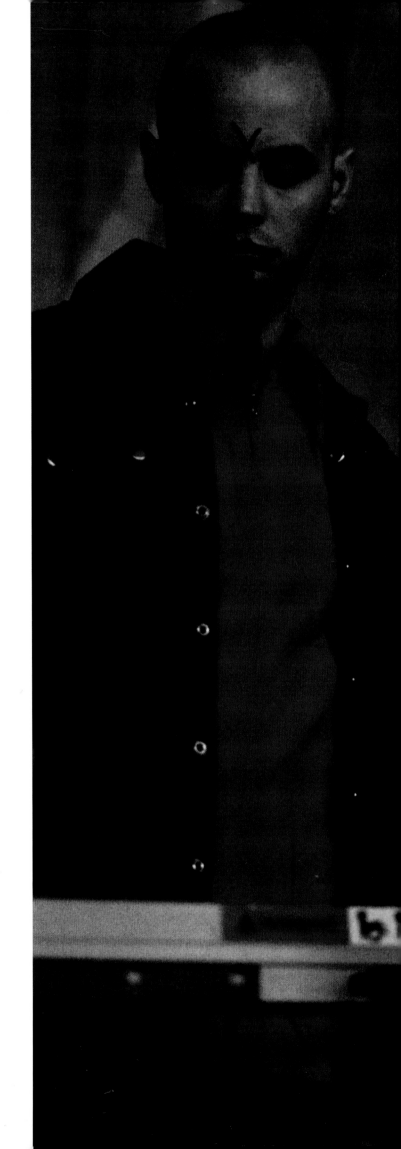

INAUGURATION

It was in May of 1993 that Trent Reznor extended the party invitation of a lifetime to Mr. Manson and his troupe. A collegiate journalism major, Manson allegedly interviewed his future mentor Reznor after a Nine Inch Nails gig in Florida, and as his own music became increasingly influential and critically acclaimed, Reznor had not failed to keep his ears pricked for other bands' sounds. Reznor's invitation to Manson that he and his band be the premiere act on his new Nothing label was fittingly extended at none other than the "Manson Mansion," the site of the horrific murder of Sharon Tate committed by the hands of the original Manson Family in 1969. Reznor had unwittingly (and if you believe that . . .) rented the house to use as his studio. Nothing Records would soon be the home of quite a few other bands, notably Coil, Meat Beat Manifesto, Prick, Pig, and the trailblazing UK group Pop Will Eat Itself, but Marilyn Manson was the very first family member, and just to make the occasion that much sweeter, Reznor threw in the opening spot on the upcoming Nine Inch Nails 1994 "Self Destruct" tour.

And so it was that the former Spooky Kids got down to business. Early publicity shots of the band show a much more colorful, much less frightening version of the fearful five. Manson can be found in red vinyl peacoat and candystripe tights clutching a lunchbox and looking for all the world like an apprehensive little kid, hair freshly brushed and parted by mom, in the driveway having his picture snapped before his first day of school. Madonna in rapper snow hat featuring the logo TWAT, Daisy looking frighteningly like Elvis Costello with long hair, and Twiggy in faux leopard-skin cap and coat over a baseball uniform complete the picture of a band packed and ready for a trip.

Capturing the showmanship and abandon of the Marilyn Manson sound on tape was not an easy task. The group set up shop at Criteria Studios in Miami to work on their first official album release, scheduled to hit the stores in July 1994. All did not, as they say, come up roses, however, and Manson was frustrated to hear the signature madman's-day-out music he'd spent years cultivating all but disappear after production and mixing were completed. The disappointing results were duly handed over to Reznor in California who took over as Executive Producer and whipped the sessions into shape. The outcome was the thirteen track collection of Manson gems entitled *Portrait of an American Family*.

The album cover, sporting a well-deserved "Parental Advisory" logo, should certainly have prepared first-time listeners for something just a little different, just a bit deranged, outrageous, and twisted. The portrait is a scene handmade by Mr. Manson featuring a doll family of four seated in their own hideously American family room. The father doll, complete with undershirt, beer, and cigarette, sports a belt buckle of a fist wrapped around a gun with the delightful logo, "Nobody Ever Raped a .38" The sleeve artwork, made up of scary Manson sketches and band photos, features a disturbed-looking young boy with a red-lipstick-smeared face clutching a needle in front of the "Manson TV"—this is Twiggy's little brother. Twiggy is listed as a band member, acknowledged for "Base Tendencies," although Gidget Gein is credited for "all bass played on this recording."

The CD itself, stamped with the "You cannot sedate all the things you hate" slogan, is a full-on, fun and fury-fueled ride on the Marilyn Manson boat to hell. As Manson knows all too well, no self-respecting kiddie watched Willie Wonka's psychedelic boat ride sequence in *Charlie and the Chocolate Factory* without feeling a little freaked out, and he brings the listener back to childhood fear with the opening track, "Prelude (The Family Trip)." It is a terrifying take on the film's scene, with Manson whispering "There's no earthly way of knowing/Which direction we are going/Not a speck of light is showing/So the danger must be growing." Suitably set up, the onslaught of samples, soundbites, warped and wonderful sounds, and songs with titles like "Organ Grinder," "Misery Machine," "Snake Eyes and Sissies," and "Wrapped in Plastic" begins.

Manson's voice growls, screams, and hisses its way through lyrics inspired by magic tricks, society's ills, Charles Manson, Willie Wonka, sex, drugs, and rock 'n' roll. The album closes with a hidden track in the form of an answering machine message recorded on the Marilyn Manson Family Intervention Hotline (407-997-9437—now sadly defunct). The voice of an infuriated woman demanding that her son be removed from the band's mailing list is the final word; she snarls, "I have already contacted the post office for your pornographic material that is being received in the mail. My next stop is my attorney." The threatening message rounds off the album with a heartfelt "Thank you and good-bye!"

The chosen single, a little dittie called "Get Your Gunn" which has as its radio-friendly subject matter the abortion issue, was written about gynecologist Dr. David Gunn who was murdered by pro-life protestors. The song, with its relentless chorus "I hate therefore I am/Goddamn your righteous hand," also appears on the soundtrack to the film *S.F.W. (So Fucking What?)*. References to just how screwed up American society has become abound on the album. The song "Lunchbox," a truly classic Manson piece, decries the horrible absurdity of the law passed eradicating metal lunchboxes as they were bound to be used as weapons—this in a country where metal detectors are in place at schools to stop kids from bringing the family pistol in for "show and tell." Manson takes on yet another persona as he sings, "The big bully try to stick his finger in my chest/try to tell me, tell me he's the best/but I don't really give a good goddamn 'cause/I got my lunchbox and I'm armed real well." The Manson recipe of nursery rhymes and heavy metal, tomfoolery and tirades, and a pinch of pins and needles is cooked up nice and hot here in the band's debut, and served American-style.

A Fallout Films promotional video to the tune of the track "Dope Hat" was produced. Directed by Tom Stern, the psychotic and psychedelic video is a visual adaptation of Willie Wonka's boat ride, with the Manson troupe, drum set and all, playing the song as they wind their way along the water. On board is a cane-wielding top-hatted Mr. Manson, a frightened boy and girl tied to their seats, and what looks to be the original Oompa-Loompas from the famed film alter-

nately rowing the boat, singing along, dancing, and pouring maple syrup onto women's bodies. After the boat has left candyland and entered the tunnel, nightmarish apparitions float by: miscellaneous pieces of fruit cut open to reveal live mice, maggots, or wriggling fish; Manson disemboweling a medical student's doll; a headless plucked chicken dancing about; a human body writhing on a flaming barbecue; and a doll whose eyes are pulled out by a pair of pliers. One particularly nasty aside is of Marilyn Manson licking drawings of people along to the subtitles, "The girls taste like girls. The boys taste like boys." Even the usually more reserved Daisy participates in a bit of scarifying facial contortions and generally gets into the spirit of things in this wild and wigged-out video which unfortunately will never see the light of VH-1 but which nevertheless is quite a piece of work.

True to form, Mr. Manson could not resist accompanying the professional, big-time manifestations of Marilyn Manson with a little homespun promotion, and hence the publication of the biggest, baddest Manson flyer yet—"The Marilyn Manson Family Reality Transmission M1 (Fall 1994)." A full-scale Declaration of Independence, Manson-style, this clever and amusing ouevre manages to pronounce the band's philosophy, provide a few good laughs, and put down the "bible-belt-wearing-pro-life-red-neck-record-burning-fundamental-fag-bashing hypocrites." Not bad for starters. It contains a proliferance of believe in yourself doctrines, claiming that "Marilyn Manson rejects conventional morality and society's self-serving standards. When WE become the majority, we will decide who 'doesn't belong.'" Charmingly illustrated with Manson sketches of syringes, razor blades, shotguns, lunchboxes, and even a "Satanic Army" van, this is nothing if not a good read. Added features are an "Advised Reading and Listening" section along with a "Things to Keep You Busy" contest. And as the world was to learn, Manson's no fool; disclaimers abound, to the tune of "Be creative. Disregard the law. Don't tell anyone we told you to" and "You must pay in responsibility. If you listen to Marilyn Manson and m!urder your family you will go to jail. That's reality. If you decide to commit suicide for a song—So Long Sucker! That kind of thinking has no place in our movement."

With an album under their collective belt, Marilyn Manson was primed and positioned to conquer the country on the coattails of none other than King of Nothing, Trent Reznor. The Nine Inch Nails "Self Destruct" tour kicked off in August 1994. Courtney Love's band Hole and the Jim Rose Circus Sideshow were also along for the ride. But what's a good nationwide tour without a spot of devil-worship and a run-in with a major religious group? Rated highly amongst the tour's highlights most certainly was the banning of Marilyn Manson from ever performing in Salt Lake City, Utah, again. As it would turn out, the Mormons didn't take kindly to Manson ripping their Bible apart on stage and flinging the holy pages upon the mosh-pit. Especially as the "Mormon Mafia" had seen him coming and had only booked innocent little Nine Inch Nails' October 18 Delta Center gig on condition that they not bring their evil friends along as support. You see, the lead singer had just been officially named a Priest of the Church of Satan by none other than head honcho Anton LaVey, with whom Manson had a summit meeting on the California leg of the tour. Mr. Manson was thereafter known as Reverend Manson, and the Mormons just weren't having it. Allegedly forfeiting the $10,000 offered to the band not to turn up, the newly ordained Reverend couldn't resist making a surprise appearance. The tour grand-finaleed its way through two nights at New York City's Madison Square Garden in mid December without a further (reported) hitch.

The Mansons decided to go Home for the Holidays, and in their ever-festive spirit celebrated the Yuletide and the New Year with four Florida gigs. And how better to add that special something to Christmastime than by a bit of joyous public exposure and an overnight stay in the slammer? The December 27 Jacksonville Club 5 concert saw the Reverend Manson arrested for "violation of the Adult Entertainment Code" by a gaggle of local cops who just happened to be in the audience. He was hustled off to the closest jail cell and not released until the next morning.

Not a month went by before another disturbance took place. Yes, it was the famed "Chicken Incident" of January 13 in Dallas, Texas, on the second night of Marilyn Manson's headlining tour with Monster Voodoo Machine as support. A chicken, requested innocently enough by the band as a joke and duly provided by the concert promoter, was let loose on stage. United Poultry Concerns, a group who despite their low profile obviously had their fingers on the pulse, immediately heard of the incident and hysterically put forth that "the audience dismembered the live chicken in a bacchanalian orgy of violence."

Well, enough on-stage upsets—how about a nationally televised Marilyn Manson transmission. To wet their chops, in February Manson, Twiggy, and Madonna Wayne Gacy were part of a discussion panel about moshing on the Phil Donahue Show, but it was the guest appearance of the Marilyn Manson crew on the *Jon Stewart Show* on June 22, 1995, the day before the talk show was canceled, that should certainly go down in TV history. The squeaky-clean talk show host announced happily to the camera, "We're ready for some music" before the set's music stage was taken over by the most colorful freak show ever to grace network television before being duly set alight. Yes, you heard right . . . Manson, never one to be caught out without a shot of lighter fluid on hand, actually set fire to the stage while belting out the "I wanna grow up/I wanna be/a big rock and roll star" chorus of "Lunchbox." The fire itself was not nearly as shocking as the onslaught of the five band members, made up and dressed up to the nines for their television appearance. The cameraman, more than likely thrilled at the departure from run-of-the-mill talk show material, followed the outrageous-as-ever Marilyn as he swooped and lunged all over the small stage. Done up in black vinyl trousers, elbow length gloves with red feather-boa trim, and only one eyebrow of sorts to speak of, Mr. Manson presented quite a contrast to the Oriental carpeted set. The unrelenting song was brought to an end by Manson attempting to destroy a mic stand and sundry equipment and the drummer collapsing on the floor behind his drum set. Fairly dramatic, but the true topper took place when Jon Stewart, in true Letterman style, came on stage to say, "There you go folks, Mar—" when he was cut off by the spidery form of Mr. Manson jumping on his back, wrapping himself around his host, attempting to pull his shirt off and covering his mouth with his begloved hands. Stewart, a good sport to be sure, took it all in stride and stamped out the fire (still burning on the floor) with his feet, while Reverend Manson enjoyed a piggyback ride. Amazingly, Stewart welcomed the pyromaniac rock star back to perform "Dope Hat" after telling the audience that before the show a roadie for the band had requested a live chicken "'cause we wanna put it in our bass drum." Warning bells may have been heard going off in a lesser talk show host's head, but hey, the show only had one more night to go.

That was not the only flame-related happening that year; earlier on during their tour the band set fire to Sarah Lee Lucas. Well, they actually lit up his drum kit, but as he was still performing at the time, the fire spread as fires are wont to do, and poor old Sarah Lee bolted from the stage still smoldering, never to return. As Twiggy would later recount to *Circus* magazine, "He sort of wasn't into it, so we never really saw him after that. I know he's alive, we didn't kill him." Manson told *Metal Edge* magazine in August 1997 that despite "the years that I had babied him during his drug addiction, and the many times that I saved his life, I only get hostility and problems from him, and so I wish him nothing but the worst." Not quite an amicable parting, but at least no one was seriously injured.

Sarah Lee's replacement, Ginger Fish (child cannibal Albert Fish and Ginger Rogers), quickly joined up. Ginger had has own rather dubious roots in the entertainment industry; his father was "a crooner who hung out with Frank Sinatra and Paul Anka" according to *Drum!* magazine and his mother a former tap dancer. He himself allegedly had a brief gig drumming in the orchestra pit for, prophetically enough, a production of *Jesus Christ Superstar*. The new drummer, however, was to endure his share of punishment as seemed to be the Marilyn Manson tradition. Fast-forward to the September 7, 1996, "nothing" night at New York City's Irving Plaza when the drummer was sent home by ambulance. Mr. Manson, as is his habit, began whipping his mic stand around wildly and lost control of it; it struck Ginger who stopped drumming for a moment or two. He began playing again only to be struck again by Twiggy's bass. The entire band reportedly left the stage—and Ginger—who crawled out from behind his drum kit before collapsing in a pool of blood before a stunned and silenced audience. Rather than the band bounding back on stage for a triumphant encore, roadies and paramedics emerged from backstage to rouse, drag away, and bandage the injured drummer. An awful way to wind up a gig, but not enough to drive Ginger to safer shores. All in day's work, apparently.

the CHILD SNATCHERS

Ginger Fish's initiation took place during Marilyn Manson's Spring tour as opening act for Danzig. Once he was suitably broken in, the band pulled off the road to record what turned out to be their first real ice-breaker into the mainstream music scene, the *Smells Like Children* EP. Named for the words of the Child Snatcher from the kiddies' film Chitty Chitty Bang Bang, the EP was intended to simply be the "Dope Hat" single, but once the band started conjuring up remixes of songs from *Portrait*, cover versions, live recordings, and a weird assortment of samples and noises, they found themselves unable to part with any of it. And wisely so. Aside from inspired originals like "S****y Chicken Gang Bang" and "Sympathy for the Parents," the EP featured a number of covers—Patti Smith's "Rock 'n' Roll Nigger" and Screamin' Jay Hawkins's "I Put a Spell on You"—but it was Marilyn Manson's version of the Eurythmics' "Sweet Dreams (Are Made of This)" that started all the trouble.

As Manson would tell *Alternative Press* in its February 6, 1997, issue, "Sweet Dreams" was "just a clever piece of cheese on a rat trap! A lot of innocuous mall shoppers bought 'Sweet Dreams' and were then introduced to this whole new world of Marilyn Manson that they didn't expect. And ultimately that's the most devious thing you could ever pull off." In the age of the MTV Nation, it was the Dean Karr–directed video for the song that brought Marilyn Manson in front of the eyes and ears of a huge audience of music fans who would otherwise not have given the band the time of day. The Manson we have come to know, love, and, in many cases, fear was suddenly on television screens across America in full costume. The image of Manson's lacerated stomach as he wandered half-dressed in a dirty tutu through empty back-streets with a crippled gait was difficult to banish from memory. Howling and whispering the Eurythmics' song through the veil of a full-length wedding dress, riding a wild pig, pounding across the floor on a pair of three-foot stilts, Marilyn Manson had crashed the party. And he wasn't going home until all the beer had been drunk and the place was a wreck.

Now was the time to pull out a few more stops. With *Smells Like Children* hung by the chimney with care, Marilyn Manson began making housecalls, visiting the hometowns of those "innocuous mall shoppers" in the hopes of further reeling them in. The first stop-off on Mission Manson was poor unsuspecting Tulsa, Oklahoma, on September 12, 1995, and the technicolor whirling dervish of a show swept across the country through Texas, New Mexico, California, Colorado, and over to the East Coast and Canada. With bands like Clutch, Hanzel and Gretyl, Halcion, and Johnny SkilSaw in tow, the Spooky Kids brought a show unlike any other to clubs in nearly all major—and quite a few minor—cities. Marilyn Manson brought in the New Year yet again, this time at New York City's The Academy with Lunachicks.

Although Manson had yet to garner any truly massive attention from the media—something not far away on the horizon—word of mouth was doing the trick. Hardcore fans and newcomers alike were deviously delighted with the matchless, shameless show that pushed itself to the extreme. Picture a wide red-lit stage fronting a crowd near-silent in anticipation. The figure of Marilyn Manson, wearing a long black cloak and a tall witch's hat is suddenly spotlit, and the eery figure's white face barely moves as he recites, in an increasingly urgent whisper, the "boat ride" segment from his beloved *Chocolate Factory*. His rasping of "the danger must be growing" reaches a peak and the band erupts into twisted, angry song.

Next up is the glam-rockesque "Dope Hat." The drum-beat-driven haunted-house opening strains are the perfect soundtrack to the silhouette of a top-hatted Manson creeping on-stage wielding a cane. Suspenders long-since shrugged off his naked coat-hanger shoulders to hang from his waist, the spider-like figure appears even more insectlike due to the bulky knee-braces on his painfully thin legs. As he jerks about the stage like a marionette controlled by a puppeteer on acid, his epileptic movements echo the song with amazing precision. Other sig-

nature stage movements for our hero include bending over backward and forward, hanging onto the mic stand for dear life, and scratching like a dog. Or the outrageous frontman might ceremoniously set a fire in a saucepan on a pedestal and then warm his hands over it like a demented hobo from another planet. To add to the otherworldly atmosphere, Manson gigs often featured a huge Ouija board backdrop, a 666 logo on speakers, a dismembered baby doll hanging from a harness, or an enormous candy cane. But all of this is just background for the band members themselves. Manson's emaciated six-foot-one-inch frame made enough of an impression on its own, but the Reverend saw fit to enhance his image with feet-high stilts and surgical braces. Daisy, ever the most conservative, might sport a Blondie T-shirt with his blue hair and ink-black eyebrows. Twiggy, looking like a doll's worst nightmare, played bass in a green and white housecoat, smeared red lipstick, false eyelashes, and a kid's candy

necklace. Pogo decorated his keyboard with what appeared to be goat and human heads. As a final mental image to take home, the audience was often treated to Manson's black vinyl thong bikini for the final encore.

And backstage? After the freak show? Little is known about the band's off-stage activities, although much can be imagined. One bizarre glimpse into the world of Marilyn Manson on the road was afforded by Twiggy, who confessed to *Circus* magazine in their July 15, 1996, issue that "I like to keep the bus clean. I just put on the Bee Gees' Greatest Hits. Not the disco stuff, but the early mod stuff. Pre-'Jive Talking' days. That was one of my pastimes on tour—put that record on and clean the bus with a duster." Well, truth is stranger than fiction. Squeaky-clean behind the scenes, the tour raged on through February 1996, at which point the band pulled back into their own world. And this time only God knew what would emerge from their bubbling cauldron.

HELL on EARTH

The only way to go was down. Set to begin work on the album that would scare the life out of the status quo, the band descended upon New Orleans, "the closest place to Hell on earth," according to Manson. Trent Reznor, in his customarily morbid style, had chosen a former funeral home as the site of his new state-of-the-art Nothing Studios. And what better spot for Marilyn Manson's newest, most dangerous experiment to date? The band set out to bring themselves to the brink of insanity, dabbling in near-death experiences and pain endurance rituals, and pushing themselves to musical and mental limits. The outcome, an album brazenly entitled *Antichrist Superstar*, was not reached without sacrifice.

Before the end of the recording venture, Daisy Berkowitz announced that he was leaving the band. Whether it was his unwillingness to go along with the band's desire to experiment musically (and otherwise) on the new album or his reluctance to dive headlong into the Marilyn Manson Land of No Return, Daisy, it seemed, had had enough. "We really tapped into the subconscious-staying up four days in a row, sleep deprivation, all sorts of unmentionable acts of self-torture. These things, I guess, were real alien to Daisy. He wasn't into making life into art. He looked at it more as a job, whereas we embraced life and art as one," Marilyn told *Guitar World* in December 1996. Although he and Berkowitz were the founding members and had made it together through the swamps of Florida to the Grand Canyon–esque brink of fame and, ideally, worldwide domination, the relationship between the two had become increasingly "turbulent." As Manson rationalized, "There's always been an element of friction there—one of those singer/guitar player tension things. But in our case, it never really jelled into a good working dynamic." Manson's official statement on the split explained that the recording of the album was "difficult as it involves many trips dangerously close to chaos. . . . Unfortunately Berkowitz had grown creatively in a different direction, and left the band as we were beginning this project. We wish him success but plan to leave this situation stronger

than ever." Daisy's own statement said, "Marilyn Manson have been together for six years and I believe that now the time is right for me to concentrate on my own music and other projects of special interest. I wish the best for Marilyn Manson." He has since been rumored to be working on a new musical venture under the name Three Ton Gate.

Wasting no time, the remaining Manson family put ads out for a new guitarist. Zim Zum, who for all intents and purposes may be a very stylish mute with killer guitar skills, remains a bit of a mystery. The only hardcore evidence that he did not drop from the heavens (or rise from the fiery depths of Hell) when Daisy retired is his documented participation in the Chicago band Life, Sex, and Death. One can't help but wonder if his not having taken the usual Marilyn Manson–esque moniker is an indication of superior or inferior standing as a fledgling. The only clue thus far is Manson's statement to *Circus* magazine that Zim Zum "joined *Antichrist Superstar* more than he joined Marilyn Manson." The name Zim Zum is certainly mysterious, and can be traced to the term for "extraction" in the Hebrew Cabala (God "extracting" himself from space in order to allow Creation to take place). As the Reverend himself put it to *Alternative Press* in February 1997, the name Zim Zum comes from that of "an angel that was created to do God's dirty work in the Old Testament days." Manson insisted that when Zim Zum auditioned, "before he even began playing I felt like he'd be the right guy. I like his confidence and his attitude." Daisy Berkowitz was credited as a writer and guitarist on the new album, with Zim Zum down as "live guitarist for Antichrist Superstar." The fact that he survived the recording sessions alone seems to be an indication that he was meant to be part of the band as they headed toward their new millennium.

The ambience in Nothing Studios must have been bizarre beyond comprehension; Twiggy Ramirez found it worth comment. As he told *Circus* in July 1996, "A lot of the staff is a little weird. A lot of them wear, I don't know if it's a uniform or what, but they wear gray wigs with clip-on ear-

rings. It's a bit odd, but I guess it's part of the atmosphere." Trent himself apparently took to donning a Quiet Riot mask whilst mixing the album. The members of Marilyn Manson added their own touch of madness—aside from the obvious of course—by setting up tents in the middle of the studio, camping out amongst the recording gear like high-tech bedouins.

As for the much-speculated upon influence of drugs on the creation of *Antichrist Superstar*, Manson is characteristically straightforward. He confessed to *Circus* magazine in its June 17, 1997, issue that there was "a seemingly never ending supply of different drugs and pills in New Orleans, and it had a certain influence on the recording process," but stressed that it was more the otherworldly atmosphere of the city that inspired the sessions in the studio, recalling that "the smell of death and decay was everywhere and it certainly crept on the album. That was the most powerful influence ever. It made us realize just how much death is a natural part of life."

The music itself on the new album is a definite departure. Slick, skillful, and ultimately scarier, it presented the fully-realized potential of the Marilyn Manson machine. As Trent Reznor said in *Spin*'s March 1997 issue, "I wanted to show that the band had some scope, that it wasn't all guitar-bass-drums." Manson told *Guitar World* magazine in December 1996 that "We wanted to go to an outside source like Trent and have him put our vision together." He went on to declare, "We were in a different state of mind when we made that record. So sometimes we're not even sure what we did. It was very stream-of-consciousness." As Twiggy mysteriously put forth to *Circus* in July 1996, *Antichrist Superstar* "was recorded in the future already, and it was sent back. So it's already done, we just have to make it so people can hear it today. Because it's not out yet. It's the future, but it's the past cause it's really all the same. The record from the future, but it's about the past—the past that hasn't happened yet."

Antichrist Superstar, released on October 8, 1996, entered the charts at Number Three, finding itself in the unlikely company of Number One and Two acts Celine Dion

and Kenny G. The sudden juxtaposition of an outfit led by a man *Guitar World* magazine called "profoundly ugly and violently disturbed" with the wholesome, soap and water goodness of the current God and Goddess of middle-of-the-road musical values caused the mainstream media to sit up and listen. Or, at least, give the freaks a cursory mention. *Entertainment Weekly*, in its October 25, 1996, edition, spotlighted the album in its Charts section, scoffing, "Antichrists, maybe; superstars, not yet," and went on to reassure their readers that the album, which they described as Manson's "latest lurid attempt to capture the hearts, minds, and school lunch money of young America," would surely drop off the charts none too soon. The only problem was that the album, which sold 132,000 copies in its first week, was actually quite good. *Rolling Stone* featured *Antichrist Superstar*—along with a ghoulish cartoon of a worm with the Reverend Manson's head winding its way through a garden of skulls and bones—in its November 28, 1996, "New Recordings" section. Awarding a respectable three and a half stars, the venerable music mag declared that the album "could make the group rock's next billion dollar babies."

The sixteen songs on the album tell the story of a worm that metamorphoses into an angel. They are divided into three segments, "Cycle I: The Heirophant," "Cycle II: Inauguration of the Worm," and "Cycle III: Disintegration Rising." These songs present an older, darker, and more serious Marilyn Manson; one whose threat to take over the world had itself undergone a metamorphosis from childlike taunt to alarming promise. Opening with the line, "I am so all-American, I'd sell you suicide," in the track "Irresponsible Hate Anthem," the album is a relentless seventy-seven minute rampage whose quieter moments are even more ominous than its screams of terror. As Manson told *Spin*, "This record is about personal strength and by seeing my own death and learning from it is where I obtain that strength."

Manson explores his own subconscious through touching upon his own experiences. The song "Kinderfeld" was inspired by his grandfather—a truck driver who, according

to family myth, was caught out upon arrival at the hospital after an accident wearing women's lingerie under his clothes—who used to masturbate while running his train set in the basement. Manson, who admitted to *Q* magazine that "just thinking about it gives me a chill," described his most recent visit to his grandmother, who still lives in the house she shared with his now-deceased grandfather, when he ventured down the basement stairs to find that "the train set was still there and there were all these rusty paint cans hanging from the ceiling. I opened them and they're still filled with 16mm porno movies." "Tourniquet" ("She's made of hair and bone and little teeth/And things I cannot speak") recounts his recurring dream of creating a companion for himself out of the his own hair and baby teeth combined with prosthetic limbs.

The album's first single, "The Beautiful People," pounded its way onto the airwaves. Manson's voice, as frightening in falsetto as in its customary hoarse howl, bombarded mainstream society and music to the beat of tribal-techno drums, putting down the so-called beautiful ones in one foul blow. The accusational cries of "Hey You, what do you see?/Something beautiful, something free?" were soon on high-rotation MTV courtesy of a gorgeously disturbing video. It was directed by Floria Sigismondi, the Italian director who is becoming known for visually presenting the dark side of the human mind. Sigismondi has also worked with the likes of Tricky and David Bowie. She told MTV News that "a lot of my images come from that time when you just go to sleep, and I usually end up writing in the dark or just when I wake up," adding, "I think it could get pretty scary if people hide that side of them, and then kind of let it out in other ways, where I'm very visible with it, and it's a safe way." Manson himself, the main inspiration behind the videos disturbing images, told MTV that he introduced Sigismondi to his fondness for "prosthetics and other medical fetishes" and that the band "all went wild with, you know, her ideas. And I think she did a great job. It did leave some bad cuts in my mouth, which unfortunately probably will never heal."

CONTROVERSY RISING

The shit hit the fan not long after *Antichrist Superstar* hit the stores. Anti–Marilyn Manson sentiments were nothing new, of course. Back in the good old days, the British church and state reportedly hoisted a campaign to ban *Portrait of an American Family* - "[British Member of Parliament] Blackburn, who is also a member of the Church of England Synod," according to the September 24, 1994 edition of the *Daily Insider*, "thinks 'It's appalling. I would ban this sort of thing tomorrow. It's breaking up society.'" But that was smalltime dissension compared to the uproar that broke out and grew to monstrous proportions by the time Marilyn Manson's "Dead to the World" tour began burning its path across America.

Antichrist Superstar was barely stocked on the shelves when Senator Joe Lieberman of Connecticut denounced local record stores for "marketing death and degradation as a twisted form of holiday cheer." Lieberman, along with "culture warriors" William Bennett of Empower America and others, confronted none other than the C.E.O. of Seagram for, according to Christopher Stern reporting for Reuters News Service on December 10, 1996, "failing to honor a promise not to distribute music with violent and profane lyrics through his MCA Music Group." Bennett reportedly held up for example the cover of the *Antichrist Superstar* CD and declared it "crap and filth." Empower America and other such ultraconservative organizations have been known to praise retail chain Wal-Mart for refusing to carry CDs of which they do not approve or for carrying them only if the cover artwork and/or lyrics are changed and special edition CDs are manufactured solely for their stores. The attack against record labels for releasing artists' music (whatever next?) and against stores that sell music, for, well, selling music, was to become a full-on battle waged even in cyberspace. The American Family Association announced on its web page that it was "endorsing a nationwide boycott of the Minneapolis-based Best Buy Company because of its sponsorship of the 'Ozzfest' tour which features hate-rock group Marilyn Manson" and issued a press release on June 20, 1997, in

which Tim Wildmon, Vice President of the A.F.A., is quoted as saying, "Best Buy's promotion of this hateful act is the moral equivalent of dealing drugs to children."

The "Dead to the World" tour 1996–97 kicked off on October 3, 1996, in Kalamazoo, Michigan, at the State Theatre. And once the show was underway, there was no stopping the madness. Marilyn Manson, the band and the man, were to take on much more than just another tour. The Antichrist Superstar was to find himself up against the Religious Right, and it wasn't going to be pretty. He was attempting to play by his rules on their turf, and when the Manson tour bus pulled into the Heartland's hometowns, that famed Southern hospitality took on a decidedly unwelcoming attitude. To say the least.

Marilyn Manson, perhaps wisely, stuck to the apparently more sympathetic North at the start of the tour, playing in Illinois, Ohio, New York, Canada, Massachusetts, Rhode Island, New Jersey (the October 31 gig which proved uneventful save a bomb threat or two and rumors of Mr. Manson's planned Halloween celebratory suicide), and Washington, D.C. The band then slipped down to the relative safety and ensured welcome of its "home state" of Florida before skipping town and leaving the good old U.S.A. to head over to Santiago, Chili, for the November 22 Close-Up Festival to play in the prestigious company of Bad Religion, Cypress Hill, and the Sex Pistols. Concerts in Sweden, Denmark, Germany, Belgium, France, Spain, and the UK followed with the band Fluffy as opening act. It was when the former Spooky Kids re-entered America with Drill and L7 as support that the simmering stew of controversy began to boil over. Oklahoma City governor Frank Keating, who MTV News described as "surprisingly knowledgeable" about "the tragically misunderstood Marilyn Manson," declared, in the face of the impending February 5, 1997 gig at the state fairgrounds, that the band is "clearly bent on degrading women, religion, and decency."

The beginning of March gave the clamoring American masses a breather again while the band's traveling show

popped over to Japan and then down to Australia and New Zealand. Mr. Manson, in good form, re-entered the States with a bang, tripping onstage in Honolulu, Hawaii, on March 22, landing on a sharp object (try falling on a Manson stage and not hitting something potentially harmful), and cutting an artery in his hand. He was rushed off to the emergency room for stitches. The incident was reported in *Billboard* magazine, which noted that "the accident apparently was not part of the show." Manson's manager reportedly "called MTV News to stress that contrary to local press reports, Marilyn did not slash his wrists intentionally during the show." Who else would, due to a horrible accident, almost die and generate immediate public opinion that the near-tragedy was in fact deliberate?

The next leg of the tour, with New York Loose, Helmet, and Rasputina (a group made up of three female cellists) as support, began on April 5 in LaCrosse, Wisconsin. Oh, and what a fuss! Glenn Walinski, director of the LaCross Center, told none other than *Rolling Stone* (June 12, 1997 issue) that the Manson concert "was the worst thing I've been through. It divided our community." The band then moved on to bring their crusade against all that is run-of-the-mill to a town called Normal, Illinois (whether it remains so is yet to be seen). Protestors turned out with bells on to show their disapproval of the April 17 concert in Jacksonville, Florida. The Associated Press released a statement from a resident of the town; a Stan Carter asserted that the rock star was "pressing hatred and dislike and violence toward Christians. This man is a slap in the face. He's no less an affront than Nazis marching down Myrtle Avenue."

The April 20 concert at the University of South Carolina Coliseum set a precedent by actually being canceled. Unable to handle the pressure "reportedly launched by state treasurer Richard Eckstrom, who first learned about the band at a church service," according to MTV News, the college and promoter Cellar Door Productions decided to call off the festivities, and came to an agreement with the band whereby Marilyn Manson would be paid the reported tidy sum of $40,000 *not* to play! A bill attempting to bar Marilyn Manson from ever performing in a state facility was also introduced by state legislators. As *Rolling Stone* reported in their on-line "Random Notes Daily" on April 14, Eckstrom felt the band was "needlessly offensive and dehumanizing." In a curiously unclear attempt to set forth the state's reasoning behind its anti-Manson stance, Treasury spokesperson Scott Malyerck was quoted as saying, "This group certainly isn't like Olivia Newton-John or Blondie, and is far afield of decent music. . . . We don't think they provide any redeeming qualities whatsoever—social, moral, or musical. And I'm a rock fan." Well, that goes without saying. What the state of the music entertainment industry would be if the main criteria for live performance was similarity to either Olivia Newton-John or Blondie (why these two artists, whose only common attribute is femaleness, have been linked in this context is not immediately evident) is difficult to speculate, but everyone is entitled to their opinion. Except, apparently, Marilyn Manson fans. Mr. Manson's response to all this? He asked MTV, "What do you expect from a state that still flies the Confederate flag?" and succinctly labeled his detractors "fascist bigots."

A Reverend Dana Wilson of Michigan not only attempted to persuade concert promoters to cancel the April 25 Wendler Arena show, but, failing to do so, went for second-best and, with a petition signed by 20,000 locals, put forth his suggestion that concert-goers under eighteen years of age not be allowed to attend the show without a parental chaperon (a concept the Reverend Manson would no doubt greet with glee).

On more than one occasion gigs were canceled due to local protestors' pressure and swiftly rescheduled in the face of ultimately more threatening legal pressure. Despite allegations that the band was "not consistent with our community standards" by Richmond, Virginia, City Manager Robert C. Bobb (a statement in itself inconsistent as some 2,000 tickets had already been sold, presumably to members of said community), the city decided that nasty old Marilyn Manson wasn't all that bad after all and reslated the previously nixed May 10 show. *Billboard*

reported on May 3, 1997, that the concert was rescheduled "after city officials realized they could be violating the band's First Amendment rights." All with a little help from the American Civil Liberties Union, who stand behind Marilyn Manson's right to perform.

Ironically, the only trouble the "Dead to the World" tour has seen has been before the shows; the concerts themselves have gone, as the band's attorney Paul Cambria told *Billboard*, "without a hitch." Booking agent Artist and Audience encourages worry-wart venue heads to check their facts by getting reports from previous concert-holders. Perhaps the most publicized hub of protest was Biloxi, Mississippi, where cries to cancel the April 12 show were particularly noisy. Bill Holmes, the director of the Mississippi Coast Coliseum, was quoted in *The Sun Herald* on March 26 as saying, "I want to cancel the show. I've got people saying I'm in bed with Satan." Interestingly, after the concert Holmes told *Billboard* that they "had no problems whatsoever" and went on to add that "We did not have one fight—not one unruly deal." Which, to anyone who has ever attended a rock concert, is quite an unheard-of statistic. Holmes was also inter-

viewed by *Rolling Stone* it its June 12, 1997, issue, wherein he noted, "We've done Alice Cooper, Judas Priest, Kiss. But this was the granddaddy—unbelievable."

Well, being railed against by notoriously excitable Bible Belters is one thing, but you'd expect bigger and better of the rock 'n' rollers in New York City, now wouldn't you? Incredibly, the latest trend in concert cancelation caught on at Giants Stadium—and even more incredibly, the venue wanted to strike Marilyn Manson from the OzzFest '97 bill on June 15. That the original king of controversy, a man famed for biting the head off of a live rat onstage in his hey day, should put together a concert featuring the likes of Pantera, Type O Negative, and a reunion of Black Sabbath and be told that "all of that is just fine, as long as you don't bring that horrible Manson fellow with you" is nothing short of insulting! Ozzy Osbourne's public statement about the unfolding situation was, "Nobody has the right to tell me who I can perform with. . . . This is not an issue of taste. It is an issue of civil liberty and freedom." Of course, Ozzy has dealt with the moral majority before, and takes it all with a sense of humor; as he told *Rolling Stone* in their May 22, 1997, "Random Notes Daily," "It makes my heart feel wonderful when I hear that these idiots are coming out of their fucking attic again. I have to laugh." On April 28 Marilyn Manson, along with concert promoter Delsener/Slater and Ardee Festivals N.J. Incorporated, filed a lawsuit against the New Jersey Sports and Exposition Authority. The Director of Giants Stadium, Bob Castronovo, was quoted in the May 3, 1997, issue of *Billboard* as stating that "we will offer [OzzFest] a contract with our parameters in them, one of which gives us the right to choose the groups [for the show]." On May 7 the courts sided with our heroes and ruled that the show would go on, and that the Authority was neither to attempt to stop Marilyn Manson from performing as part of the concert nor to obstruct ticket sales in any way. The final word on the OzzFest? *Billboard Bulletin* July 9, 1997, ran an article entitled "OzzFest is a Surprise Success Story," noting that "the nine shows with shock rock act Marilyn Manson were among the most successful, includ-

ing crowds of 32,500 in Minneapolis and 32,000 in Milwaukee." As Manson himself told *Metal Edge* magazine in its August 1997 issue, the OzzFest was "great, it's kind of like the old school coming together with the new school, because I know Ozzy's gone through a lot of the same things that I'm going through right now."

Well, there's nothing like a bit of outrage and protest mixed with rock 'n' roll to fire up the media. Not to be left out of a sensational story in the making, *Rolling Stone* featured a stamp across its June 12 cover reading "The Plot Against Marilyn Manson." The article itself, entitled "How the Christian Right is trying to run Marilyn Manson off the road" was a veritable *Sixty Minutes*–style research into the convoluted and truly incredible trail of anti-Manson propaganda. Conservative groups such as the American Family Association, the Christian Family Network, Empower America, and the Oklahomans for Children and Family were reported to be circulating so-called factual information on the band via the mail, fax, and most rampantly over the Internet, including "affidavits" detailing common occurrences at Manson gigs such as "animal sacrifices, sex with dogs, rapes, and heavy drug use," to name but a few.

The American Family Association's official web page boasted an entire section devoted to "Marilyn Manson Info" (info being an abbreviation for information, apparently in the broadest sense of the term), featuring "Media Reports & Eye-Witness Accounts of recent concerts," "Things Parents and Youth Ministers need to know about Marilyn Manson," and the "National Clearinghouse on Marilyn Manson Concerts for Family & Decency Advocates." Yet another unfounded anti-Manson claim was to be found in the A.F.A.'s June 20, 1997, on-line press release which noted that "the band's music has been tied to at least two teen suicides." The enthusiasm with which these reports were broadcast and distributed (to the police, churches, schools, state and local governments) and the eagerness with which they were taken as gospel truth was truly astounding.

The fervor stopped short, however, at the notion of verifying the accuracy of any of the disinformation.

The A.F.A.'s Manson-related activities and web site prompted the formation of The Portrait of An American Family Association and its own inspired website dedicated to spreading the down-and-dirty truth about Marilyn Manson, its music, concerts, and Mr. Manson's message. The Washington State Chapter of the P.O.A.A.F.A. states on its web page that "it is our goal to put an end to the outrageous rumors and slanders that have plagued this band since its release of the *Antichrist Superstar* CD. By doing this we hope to prevent the banning of further Marilyn Manson concerts so that others can choose for themselves if they desire to support or criticize this unique band." The logical, responsible, and well-researched P.O.A.A.F.A. web page urges Manson fans to respond to false accusations about the band by e-mailing, faxing, writing, and otherwise spreading the word to the likes of the A.F.A. and other church and government organizations, cautioning fans to "be polite but tell the truth," and offers an educational flyer for downloading. If a Manson fan encounters a protestor outside of a concert, he is encouraged by the P.O.A.A.F.A. to keep a stiff upper lip in the face of fanatical chanting and offer the flyer (entitled "Marilyn Manson Facts: What the religious right *doesn't* want you to know" and written by none other than angelynx–a.k.a. Paula O'Keefe–a high-profile, intelligent, and articulate fan and on-line contributor to many a Marilyn Manson web page) as a retort.

Marilyn Manson himself, who has never been known to give the proverbial rat's ass what people say about him, even began to get a little pissed off at the preposterous claims of the self-appointed guardians of America's pseudo-morals. He doesn't mind a bit of dissension—in fact he applauds it—but would prefer for it to be remotely reality-based. As he told *Rolling Stone* in its June 26, 1997, issue, "I don't have a problem with someone who opposes me or wants to try and stop a show because they think that Marilyn Manson contributes to the decay of Western civilization, or if someone doesn't want to buy an album

because they think it sucks. But these people didn't just disagree with my message. They completely *ignored* my message." In his first public retort to some of the Internet-posted "reports" of his gigs, he puts himself across as much more reasonably minded than his detractors. To claims that he kills puppies on stage he states, "I like dogs. I have a dog." To allegations that he has a squad of "private Santa Clauses" who distribute drugs to the audience, he scoffs, "That is ridiculous. If I had a giant bag of drugs, I would not be passing them out, especially for free. I would be backstage doing them." Of the various violent and sexual acts of which he has been accused, Manson has often queried how he is supposed to have performed such deeds - some of which are felonies - in front of thousands of people without being handcuffed and carted off to the Big House. Indeed, video-camera-wielding but inevitably disappointed members of many a police department have allegedly presided over Manson concerts in the hopes of catching an illegal act or two on tape to no avail.

To protest that his on-stage persona and behavior is outrageously indecent and offensive, Manson has an unperturbed commonsense rebuttal. "Some of it might be tasteless for some people, but then who told them to look?" he asked *Circus* magazine in June of 1997. "I don't know if it's tasteless or not, a lot of it is exciting to me. I do whatever I want, I'm discovering myself on and off stage." With an intuitive leap of reasoning, Manson has even managed to turn the tables on the likes of the A.F.A., stating in the August 1997 issue of *Metal Edge*, "It's ironic to me because these people have taken such an interest in pornography and filth and deviant behavior, that they've obtained the ability to dream up some very perverted fantasies, and I think if they're pointing the finger at me being sick, they should look at who's making up the stories." In fact, Manson actually mourns the loss of innocence; as he told *Metal Hammer* in July 1997, "In America, nothing excites anybody anymore. I'd have loved to have lived in a time when looking up a girl's skirt was exciting." On the other hand, he adds, "If it will make people happy to experiment sexually, then fine, that'll make me happy, because I like

to hear of people doing more than sitting in front of the TV and doing the acceptable."

As for the band's documented views on religion, they are decidedly straightforward. "Going to confession and being 'clean' afterwards is not our idea of how it should work. It helps people to avoid responsibility," Twiggy Ramirez explained to *Circus* magazine in its May 20, 1997, issue. Manson admitted to *Guitar World* in December 1996, "I'm very much opposed to Christianity, but most of my values are something that Jesus might have preached" and told *Spin* that the *Antichrist Superstar* album "will be America's God's punishment for the sins that they've created for themselves, and hopefully, I'll be remembered as the person who brought an end to Christianity." "Because we tell people that we are against organized religions doesn't mean we burn down churches or worship the devil. We have our own religion and some parts of it are even identical with some Christian beliefs," Twiggy told *Circus*. As Manson summed it up to *Metal Edge* in August 1997, "America has left a very dirty taste in my mouth when it comes to the idea of God."

At times, however, Mr. Manson seemed to take it all with a pinch of salt, keeping in mind that age-old showbiz adage that there's no such thing as bad publicity, reasoning that "if people really care about fighting off so-called 'problems' like Marilyn Manson, they would actually choose to ignore us. The more they bitch about us, the more attention they give us." "I thought we were in a different day and age where people were intelligent enough to understand art and music. Apparently that's not the case," he quipped to *Metal Edge* in August 1997. However, his core view on the situation is that it is a serious one indeed. As he told *Metal Edge* in its August 1997 issue, "It's just gotten to the point where I feel like I'm the only one fighting for rock music in general, because these people are just trying to take away my right—to take away everyone's right—to not only hear what they want but to say and do what they're entitled to under the First Amendment. It's become a full-on revolution for me." Well, isn't that just what he wanted? A revolution? And true to his prophetic word, that's just what he's got.

ANGELWORMS

In keeping with the original Marilyn Manson ethic of celebrating the opposing extremes of life, just as many people adored Manson and his music as despised him. As Manson put it to *Alternative Press* in its February 6, 1997, issue, "I've always found that there are two kind of people in the world; people who like Marilyn Manson and people who are jealous." In fact, some factions of society found him extremely entertaining. Antichrist aside, he has most certainly become a superstar, and anyone who looks like that and gives a hell of an interview deserves a bit of attention.

Turning up here, there, and everywhere, Marilyn Manson and his cohorts soon found themselves in the public eye like never before. Awards were no longer confined to the microcosmic Slammies. The "Sweet Dreams" video found itself up against seasoned professionals like Metallica in the MTV Awards. In 1996 Marilyn Manson was inducted into Cleveland's Rock 'n' Roll Hall of Fame. *Hit Parader*'s 1997 Reader Survey saw Marilyn Manson voted "Favorite Band." Mr. Manson's photo began surfacing in publications of all description. He was snapped standing next to Billy Corgan, making even the Smashing Pumpkins frontman look like a suntanned picture of health. *Spin*'s Special Twelfth Anniversary Issue "The SPIN 40" featured a suitably disturbed-looking Manson, complete with dead duck, as number 22, dubbing our hero "one scary monster, one super creep." Praise indeed.

Rumors began making their fast and furious way through the undergrowth: Manson to commit suicide on Halloween, Manson will be having a single breast implant, Manson spread blood on a baby while giving an autograph (he claims it was lipstick), Manson cut off his own testicles. Manson engaged in a sex act on stage with Nine Inch Nails guitarist Robin Finck while his parents were in the audience. And, of course, perhaps the most famed rumor of all . . . as Mr. Manson himself put it to *Metal Edge*, August 1997, "People

said that I removed my two bottom ribs so that I could perform oral sex on myself. But that's untrue. The operation was far too expensive."

Manson, with date Twiggy Ramirez, turned up at Howard Stern's *Private Parts* February 28, 1997, premiere party at New York's Madison Square Garden. The Reverend Manson looked quite respectable—relatively speaking—in suit and tie, and was quoted as professing to tune in to the King of All Media's show "when I've been up all night doing drugs." The *Private Parts* soundtrack, boasting acts such as AC/DC and Porno for Pyros, has its requisite Marilyn Manson original in the song "The Suck for Your Solution." Party guests included Rob Zombie, Robin Quivers, Manson who was accompanied, according to *Spin* magazine, by a blonde "nude masseuse," Conan O'Brien, Joey Buttafucco and his lawyer . . . the list goes on. Manson reportedly partied on until the wee hours with fellow rock stars Billy Corgan, Anthrax, Alice in Chains, and Perry Farrell. At the Thirty-ninth Annual Grammy Awards in April, Rob Zombie was interviewed before the show and was quoted in *Rolling Stone* as declaring, "Some of the guys in Nine Inch Nails and Marilyn Manson are back at the hotel. We're all gonna watch it there—that's how it'll be fun." Difficult as it may be to imagine Trent, Twiggy, and gang snuggled up in their jammies in front of the set eagerly awaiting some room-service beers to arrive, we have to take Mr. Zombie's word for it. Manson even made his big screen debut in who other than David Lynch's film *The Lost Highway*. His part? A porno star, of course. He and Twiggy appeared in the opening scene of the film, in which Manson is naked and dead. So, it seemed, the Reverend Manson was quite capable of hanging out with the beautiful people after all. Of course, infiltration is always a spy's first mission, and how better to meet new allies?

As press coverage rose to a fevered pitch in the States, the UK was forced to sit up and take a bit of notice of the Manson crew. For a nation of sharp-tongued and dry-wit-

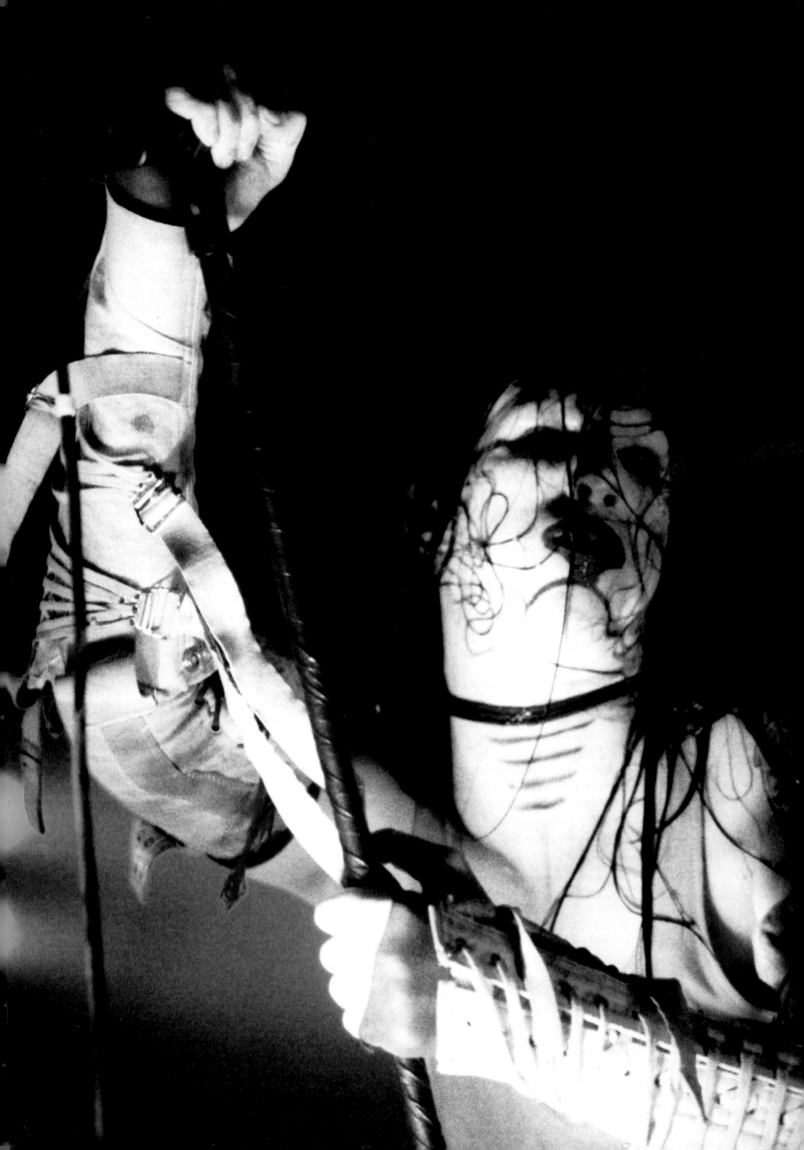

ted music critics for whom cynicism is a career requirement, the Reverend Manson got off fairly lightly. *Q*, the self-professed "World's Greatest Music Magazine" featured a large photo of the band members posing in all their glory around a hospital stretcher with Manson, scarred and lacerated chest suitably bared, in the foreground seated in a wheelchair. The photo's caption read, "No way is their image contrived." A smaller live shot of Mr. Manson live onstage in his usual garter-belt and medical-brace regalia is captioned "He's got a girlfriend, you know." The article alternately refers to our hero as "not unlike a rack-stretched Iggy Pop in Alice Cooper garb" or a "pansticked taboo-smasher."

In fact, the European music scene seems to find Manson and Company quite palatable. Either that, or they haven't taken him seriously enough yet to realize what they have on their hands. At the Dynamo Festival in Eindhoven, Holland on May 18, the band performed with the like-minded likes of Type O Negative, Entombed, Cradle of Filth, Fear Factory, Helmet, and Korn. The official Dynamo Festival T-shirts rather unfortunately listed "Marilyn Monroe" as one of its participants. The UK heavy metal magazine *Metal Hammer*'s review of the gig noted that Mr. Manson "attacked" Zim Zum "in a fit of murderous intent" and that after the lead singer incited a mud fight "a great slop of shit smacked him straight in the mush." Even this sympathetic publication felt obliged to poke a little fun. The article header in the magazine's July 1997 issue read, "Ever seen your grandfather in French underwear, barking like a dog? Mr. Manson has. Some people have all the fun, eh, readers?"

The big question to most overseas media seems to be, "What is all the fuss about?" *Q* bemusedly reports that "America's neo-right have responded to this oddly childlike entertainment by taking the singer very seriously indeed." And *Metal Hammer* queries, "But what is it about Marilyn Manson that so many people in America have found so objectionable? To British eyes, the motley Manson entourage can easily be contained as a nightmare Jane's Addiction on an Alice Cooper trip. Bizarre certainly, but dangerous? Hardly." Well, that remains to be seen.

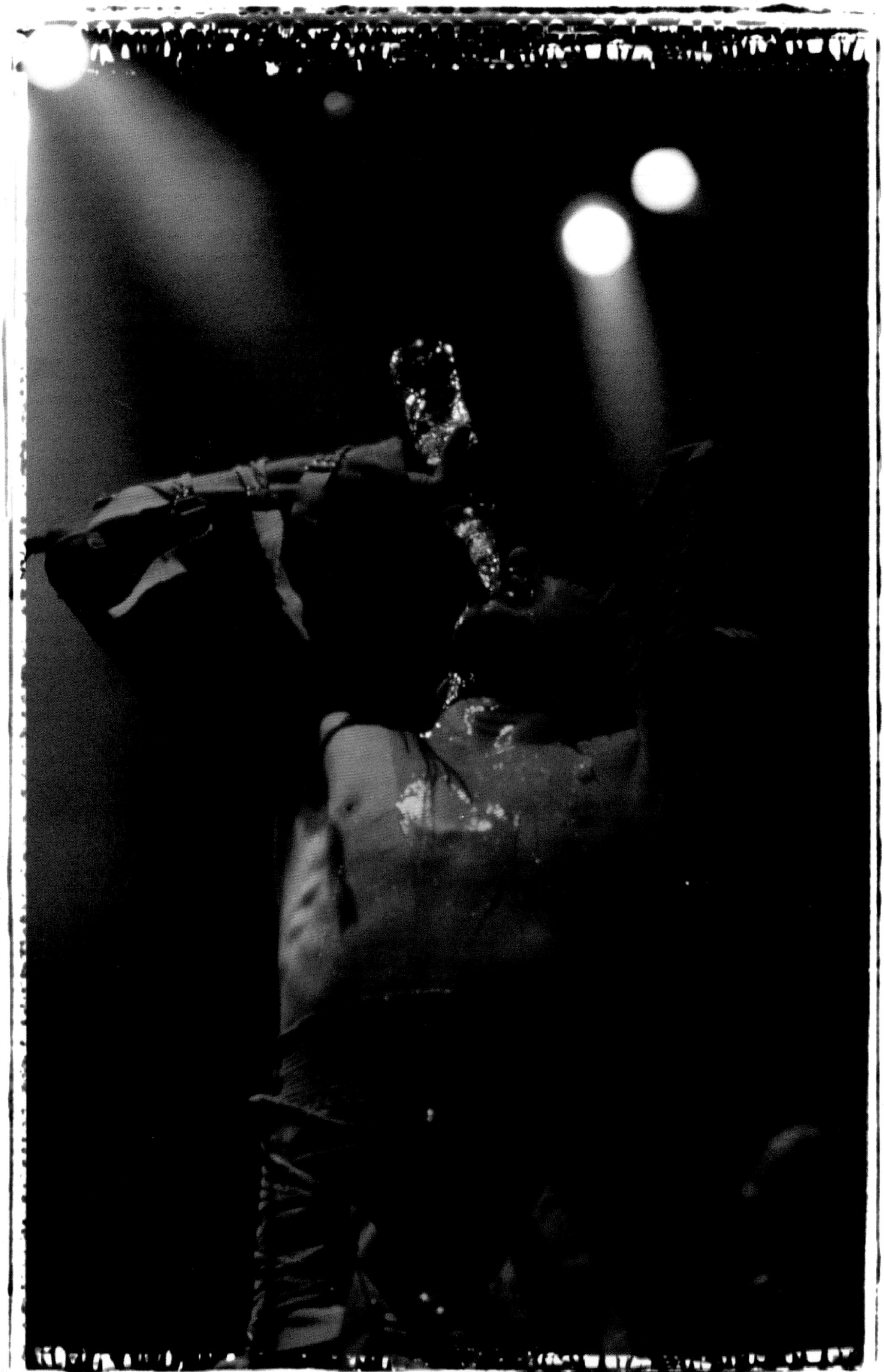

COPS and QUEERS

In the time-honored spirit of the Marilyn Manson school of thought, the troupe left the dark underbelly of New Orleans far behind and leapt headlong into the spotlight-bright glitz and glamour of Hollywood in order to create their next vision.

Mechanical Animals was Manson's triumphant stepping out from the alleged mentorship of Trent Reznor, and the evolving sound of the new and improved Marilyn Manson was met with near-unanimous critical acclaim upon its September 1998 release. Manson's heightened profile saw the album reviewed in mainstream media; *Newsweek* called it "wickedly engaging" and *Rolling Stone* declared it "an album that reassures his followers that he still belongs to them, and they to him." As Manson himself told *Rolling Stone* in its September 2, 1998 issue, "A lot of people may say this record is over the top, pretentious, and theatrical, but that's what rock music is supposed to be about."

He described the album to MTV on December 3, 1997, saying, "If *Antichrist Superstar* was sort of my comparative fall from grace, Lucifer being kicked from heaven, this next record is about what happens on Earth now. (It's about) sort of trying to fit into a society that thinks it's full of emotions and that you're a callous person, when in fact you're the one that actually has all these feelings and it's the world that's kind of numb to them. It's almost the antithesis of what I just did."

"A lot of the record is a reflection of our moving to Hollywood. We wanted to have a California record," Twiggy told *Guitar World* in its November 1998 issue. "Just living up in the Hollywood Hills, you look out on Los Angeles at nighttime and it's almost like you're on top of the world. But you're kind of alone. And that has to do with stardom, too: the loneliness thing. Before we felt alone because nobody knew who we were. Now we feel alone because everybody knows who we are... Being popular is a different kind of isolation."

In the tradition of David Bowie, Manson adopted a persona —whom he christened Omega—for the album and duly put to rest on a web cast in which he avowed, "The character of Omega has been disposed of, as he was a ruse to lure commercial mall goers into the web of destruction that I've always planned since the beginning."

Commercial mall goers were indeed lured, and this time on a grand scale. The irresistible glam-goth-rock extravaganza that was *Mechanical Animals* proved to be the proverbial Halloween apple complete with razor blade. The album debuted at a victorious Number One on the *Billboard* charts, selling some 223,000 copies in its first week. The magnificent videos for "The Dope Show" and "I Don't Like the Drugs (But the Drugs Like Me)" established Manson as not only a groundbreaking controversial artist, but also as a bona fide Rock Star, and the kids were eating it up hook, line, and sinker. The two clips kicked the shit out of the other offerings on high rotation MTV, and earned the band two *Billboard* Video Music Awards, including the Maximum Vision Award for "The Dope Show." Suddenly, Marilyn Manson wasn't hiding under the bed anymore— the monster was well and truly out of the closet.

As he put it in a February 1, 2001 conversation with *Interview* magazine, "I'm an anomaly in that I am as famous as Madonna, but I'm not a pop artist that sells gazillions of records. What I do is very counterculture, but at the same time I myself am very much pop culture, so I'm in a really strange place. I enjoy it because now I can juxtapose me against me; I become part of my criticism."

In fact, Manson decided to debunk all of the myths and offered up his autobiography *The Long Hard Road Out of Hell*. Written with journalist Neil Strauss and published by Regan Books (publisher of Howard Stern's two tomes), the brutally honest book attained the enviable status of *New York Times* bestseller. The *Washington Post*'s March 23, 1998 review declared, "It's almost worth the price of the book just to see kiddie photos of the man whose ghoulish

appearance has struck so much fear into the hearts of conservative Christians everywhere." At once repulsive and riveting, it takes the reader along for a ride through a life often aptly described as hell. Childhood recollections therein involve naked games of "Prison" with a neighbor and excruciatingly disturbing accounts of discovering his cross-dressing grandfather's filth-encrusted porn-and-dildo-filled basement hideaway complete with a personal collection of women's lingerie and wigs and mail-order bestiality shots. Truth, as they say, is stranger than fiction.

But fiction can be more fun. The prosthetic breasts Manson donned for the "The Dope Show " video and the *Mechanical Animals* cover (the androgynous image of which loomed over New York City's Time Square on an enormous billboard) prompted excitable reports that the singer had actually had breast implants. He happily embraced the enhancement theory, explaining away his subsequent lack of boobage by confessing to having the implants taken out due to excessive attention from his band mates.

There was much fuss over the Manson/Reznor "break-up." November 19, 1998's *Rolling Stone* noted that the new album dispelled "any notions that Manson was a mere acolyte of Goth-industrialist Trent Reznor, doomed to forever replicate his label boss' sound even as he surpassed him in popularity." Manson himself was not surprised by the plethora of Reznor references, telling September 2, 1998's *Rolling Stone*, "People probably expect us not to be able to function without the heavy hand of Trent. Not that I have a chip on my shoulder or need to prove something, but I think this record establishes that we have our own musical identity without someone telling us what to do."

A kiss and make up of sorts took place—appropriately enough for two rock stars, on stage—during a sold-out Nine Inch Nails gig at Madison Square Garden on May 9, 2000. They cemented it all by Manson's appearance in and direction of the NIN "Starfuckers" video. The resurrection of the friendship of a pair of controversial musical luminaries

seemed to touch one and all; the very next day Business Wire giddily reported on the on-stage reunion, calling it "a spectacular rock 'n' roll finale...ending what had become one of the most publicized spats in recent music history." The love-hate relationship seemed to swing back to the latter at some point, however, and Manson told *Rolling Stone* on September 22, 2004 that despite the NYC PDA, "Since then, he's made remarks that I don't care to respond to. And as long as I'm paying his bills, he should be respectful of me."

That split wasn't the only one centered on the creation of *Mechanical Animals*. Guitarist Zim Zum, credited as a co-writer on eight of the 12 tracks on the album, left the band before its release. He was quickly replaced by one

John 5 who is listed on the album's artwork as a band member and—echoing Zim Zum's own takeover for Daisy Berkowitz—as "Live Guitarist for *Mechanical Animals*." The fifth musician to join the band, John 5 (nee John Lowery but immediately re-christened by Manson) had sharpened his axe with extensive session work for film and TV and had played with an impressive roster of musicians such as Rob Halford, Cheap Trick's Robin Zander, David Lee Roth, and kd lang. A self-professed Manson fan long before he signed on, the talented player enthusiastically filled Zim Zum's platform shoes.

Zim Zum released a statement on July 22, 1998 saying, "We worked really hard on *Mechanical Animals* and throughout that time—creatively—a lot of doors opened for me. I looked through them and liked what I saw—so I felt it was better for me to pursue that vision." On the subject of the guitarist's departure, Manson told September 2, 1998's *Rolling Stone*, "We had problems with him not showing up, and I took that as an insult. That's just the way I am. My feelings are, if you're gonna lead a rock 'n' roll lifestyle, don't let it affect your work. I know I can stay up all night and still come in the next day and write a song, and nothing will stop me from doing it. I expect the same from everyone else."

He didn't need to worry about the band's new member's ability to deal with the lifestyle. John 5 was a self-professed perfectionist who didn't drink, smoke, or do drugs. His most perverse dirty little hobby was a penchant for practicing bluegrass guitar by day. While 5 confessed to being concerned about the other band members, he also recognized that they didn't let anything interfere with their work. "I worry that something really bad is going to happen. Seriously, I fear for those guys 'cos they party harder than anybody I've ever seen in my life. With these guys, every night is like New Year's Eve. And I just don't want someone to die. I don't want the band to be over," he told *Kerrang!* in November 2000. Manson wryly addressed the drug issue on Bill Maher's hit TV show *Politically Incorrect*, saying, "I

think drugs can also work as a bit of social Darwinism. It kind of weeds out the—you know, a lot of people that abuse drugs make the people that use them look bad. And I try to look my best." "What I like about Manson is that he works so hard. He's always writing or working on something. It's really inspiring to see so much fire and so much hunger, with the success that he's had," 5 raved in *Guitar World*'s January 2001 issue, going on to say, "They can party, man...but when Twiggy gets up later on that day, he'll be ready to work. Completely clear-headed. No problem. I don't party or anything, but if I even stay up with those guys, I'll be out of commission for days. I don't know how to do it. They must be not human. They must be made of steel or something."

The band, complete with its new clean-living axe man, set out on a whirlwind promotional tour in support of *Mechanical Animals'* success, hitting US stages in October and November before heading to Europe, Japan, and Australia in the New Year. They then launched a big-time all-arena tour with co-headliners Hole. Courtney Love & Co. were riding high on the performance of their *Celebrity Skin* album, the Manson crew were at an all-time high—what could go wrong? Well, two weeks into the "Rock is Dead" tour, the quickie marriage had crashed and burned its way to an even quicker divorce, and Hole jumped ship. And they looked so good together...

"I have two very distinct sides to me. One can be very mean; one can be very nice," Manson confessed in the April 1, 1999 issue of *What* magazine. "I usually give back to people what they give me. If a little kid is bothering me too much by crying, I give them something to cry about. It's only fair."

Melissa Auf Der Maur, Hole's glamorous bass player, weighed in on Hole's early departure from the ill-fated joint tour in a May 10, 1999 interview with the *Boston Herald*, saying, "I hear people say that Manson fans were booing us. No, that would not drive us off a tour. If anything the

arena setting made us work a little harder, because we hadn't ever had to translate everything, from our stage moves to our songs, in such a big space. We hadn't done that often, so it was a challenge, but nobody was booing us. It was just a financial disaster for many reasons." The main reason, one would speculate, being that Hole was responsible for 50 percent of the production costs of the co-headlining tour, the majority of which appeared to go towards the pyrotechnics, props, wardrobe, and God knows what else it took to create Marilyn Manson's dramatic set. It was widely reported, however, that it wasn't an asymmetrical budget that was to blame, but rather an increasingly vicious feud between the two co-stars. Onstage taunts—lobbed out mainly by Mr. Manson—were nightly occurrences, and he didn't confine his acerbic commentary to the stage, either, blithely dissing Hole and in particular the lovely Ms. Love in the press. "It looks as if she's doomed to play dead celebrities' middle-aged wives. I suppose with a little more plastic surgery she could be Yoko Ono, because she sure has the voice for it," Manson posted on marilynmanson.net. "I asked myself what is the last band in the world I would ever, ever want to tour with, and it was Hole, beyond a doubt. But then I thought, I love a challenge, I like to surround myself with aggravation, it helps me perform better," he told the *San Francisco Examiner*, saying that the tour would give him the opportunity to "show Courtney the difference between being a celebrity and being a real rock star." "It was primarily a business thing," Auf Der Maur insisted in the *Boston Herald*, but went on to admit, "And then, on top of it, there was a lot of bratty behavior. None of that was too serious. They've been our casual social buddies for years, so it wasn't like we took any of that personally." Hmmm.

The Hole fiasco would prove to be a minor blip on the "Rock is Dead" tour, however. In true "the show must go on" spirit, the tour persevered—taking a brief hiatus after Manson did some real damage to his ankle due to an onstage injury—before coming to a screaming, screeching halt. An homage to the ultimately doomed tour was to rise

from its ashes in the form of a live CD entitled *The Last Tour on Earth* which *Rolling Stone* branded "good, dirty fun" that "capture[s] Manson's inimitable talent for spectacle."

No one could have imagined what lay ahead for Marilyn Manson. The bandleader and his music may have reached hitherto unimagined heights with the success that *Mechanical Animals* had achieved, but little did Manson know what he was in for next. Arguably the most bizarre chapter in his life lay ahead…

IRRESPONSIBLE HATE ANTHEM

Columbine. On April 20, 1999, two students of Columbine High School in Littleton, Colorado, shot and killed a teacher and 12 fellow students before turning their guns on themselves. In the horrified aftermath of media speculation, it was widely disseminated that the two teenagers, Eric Harris and Dylan Klebold, were Marilyn Manson fans and presto—the giant but seemingly effortless leap was made: It was the music that made them do it. Manson may just as well have marched into that high school with a gun himself. Parents the world over who had never before heard of Marilyn Manson were pointing their furious fingers at the evil rock star. Despite subsequent reports that the two boys didn't actually like Manson's music, it was too late. Columbine and Marilyn Manson were inextricably bound together, forever more. Overnight, Manson had become Public Enemy Number One.

Manson responded to the influx of media requests with a brief statement that read, "It's tragic and disgusting anytime young people's lives are taken in an act of senseless violence. My condolences go out to the students and their families." He finally made more extensive public comment on the tragedy in a self-penned article in the May 28, 1999 issue of *Rolling Stone*, stating, "I chose not to jump into the media frenzy and defend myself, though I was begged to be on every single TV show in existence. I didn't want to contribute to these fame-seeking journalists and opportunists looking to fill their churches or to get elected because of their self-righteous finger pointing. They want to blame entertainment? Isn't religion the first real entertainment?"

Manson canceled the last five dates of the "Rock is Dead" tour in the wake of the shootings, posting an explanation on his website which said, "People are trying to sort out what happened and to deal with their losses. It's not a great atmosphere to be out playing rock 'n' roll shows, for us or the fans." He went on to comment, "The media has unfairly scapegoated the music industry and so-called goth kids and has speculated—with no basis in truth—that artists like myself are in some way to blame. This tragedy was a product of ignorance, hatred, and an access to guns."

Manson also postponed the release of the video for "Coma White" for six months. The clip, filmed in February and eventually released to MTV in August, was a reenactment of JFK's assassination played out by Manson and his girlfriend Rose MacGowan. Manson described it on his website as "a pageant where I used the assassination of JFK as a metaphor for America's obsession and worship of violence …my statement was always intended to make people think of how they view, and sometimes, participate in these events. Little did I know that the tragedy at Columbine and the accidental death of JFK, Jr. would follow. But it was telling to see the media shamelessly gorge itself on these events, which ultimately made my observations in the video even truer than I had originally imagined."

"When you have these kids that are angry and they have something to say and no one's listening, the media sends a message that if you do something loud enough and it gets our attention then you will be famous for it," Manson reasoned on *The O'Reilly Factor*. "Those kids ended up on the cover of *Time* magazine; the media gave them exactly what they wanted, and that's why I never did any interviews when that happened—when I was getting blamed for it—because I felt that I would be contributing to what I found to be reprehensible."

Indeed the majority of Manson's public reflection on Columbine took place years later. "It was because we weren't at a time of war and there was no identifiable villain. I had asserted myself as an artist who would challenge popular notions of right and wrong. I do and say what I want, and people are scared by that. Pointing the finger at me was inevitable," he told London's *Independent* on April 21, 2003.

Manson's articulate turn in the 2002 award-winning documentary *Bowling for Columbine* was met with surprise by many of his detractors. "Do you know how many people have come up to me and said, 'Jeez I didn't know you were so intelligent.' And I say to them, 'I didn't know you were so fucking stupid, but that's 'cos I just met you,'" he ranted in the March 2004 issue of *i-D* magazine. In a May 2003 *Blender* interview he expressed the same sentiment, perhaps even more humorously, saying, "People say, 'Wow, I'm so surprised how well-spoken you are.' It's like me saying, 'Wow, I'm so surprised that you don't smell like dog shit.'" One can see how many found it hard to reconcile the eloquent social commentator with the "God of Fuck." Manson debated the virtues of the F word with Bill O'Reilly during an appearance on *The O'Reilly Factor*, positing, "I think sometimes when you're making a point—I don't think that my lyrics are over laced with profanity because I myself

don't speak using a lot of profanity in normal conversation—but I think when you're making something aggressive and you need to get a point across, if you're angry, sometimes profanity is necessary. It's better to use a curse word than to hurt somebody else, I find."

Bowling for Columbine was a welcome forum for Manson to—yes, very intelligently—express his view on the tragedy and his association with it in many people's minds. "The two byproducts of that whole tragedy were violence in entertainment and gun control...the President was shooting bombs overseas, yet I'm a bad guy," he put forth in his measured tones to filmmaker Michael Moore. "I definitely can see why they would pick me because I think it's easy to throw my face on a TV because I'm—in the end—sort of a

poster boy for fear because I represent what everyone's afraid of because I do and say what I want."

The foaming-at-the-mouth brand of enthusiasm behind blaming Marilyn Manson was met with more tempered cries of, "Oh, come on," by many. Op ed pieces in countless newspapers and magazines pointed out the abject absurdity of believing that a rock star's music was the stimulus that spurred two kids into murderous and suicidal acts. "The only thing certain from these idiotic reports about the music–Littleton connection was that these breathless reporters and their editors had never heard of goth music prior to the shootings. If they had, they might have paused from their hysteria and asked why there haven't been other goth music-inspired murders in the 15 years or so this style has been around," Larry Katz fumed in his April 28, 1999 piece entitled "Don't Blame Marilyn Manson" in the *Boston Herald.*

But blame him they did, and with near-hysterical vigor. Manson holed himself up at home, barricading himself away from the media maelstrom and a barrage of death threats. "I was genuinely scared for my life," he said. "Initially, I thought it was another publicity stunt," *Alternative Press'* editor Robert Cherry told Knight Rider/Tribune News Service on December 18, 2000. "But the more I read about him, the more he seemed really concerned that something was going to happen to him. People latch onto half-truths, and all of a sudden he was on TV, getting blamed for this. Those first images stay with people. He's always been an easy target, and he's always made himself one. This time, it backfired on him."

"I just saw how all these people around me were feeling and the frustration really, really hit me," Manson said in a December 1, 2000 MTV interview. "That was the thing that hit me most about Columbine. Not just the victims, not just the shooters, but how it affected everyone. America was too focused on who was to blame, how many memorials we can have, but they weren't listening to what the real problem was: that there needs to be more conversations, that there are people who are really upset, and no one cares."

At the end of May, just a month after the Columbine shootings, Washington addressed the issue of violence and the country's young people, with Congress energetically debating the matter via a slew of proposed amendments. Most extreme was Republican Senator and House Judiciary Committee Chairman Henry Hyde's proposal to make the selling of entertainment (music, film, video games, books) deemed violent and sexual to people under the age of 17 a crime. "The entertainment industry gets away, literally, with murder," Hyde said in the *New York Times.* "Anybody who doesn't think rotten movies, rotten rap lyrics, rotten video games aren't poisoning—toxically poisoning—our kids' minds and making some kids think that's acceptable, just isn't paying attention." The measure was voted down, thankfully deemed unconstitutional, although the focus on the entertainment industry rather than the gun control issue could certainly be construed as a classic diversionary tactic.

Everyone, everyone, everyone had an opinion—and a strong one—about Marilyn Manson. Senator Joe Lieberman declared, "This is perhaps the sickest group ever promoted by a mainstream record company." Johnny Lee Clary, former leader of none other than the Ku Klux Klan, devoted a more-than-zealous section of his official website to the topic: "The Truth About Marilyn Manson" in which he doesn't mince words. "Madman Marilyn Manson is as guilty for the Columbine High School Massacre as the two maniacs who pulled the triggers. His music incited the killers to violence," he proclaimed. Photographs of two of the Columbine victims appear below a blazing headline "Manson Murdered These Two Little Girls" with the brazen byline "It was because of his influence and telling those two killers at Columbine to murder Christians that these two little girls lost their lives." Incredible, but indicative of the all-time high of the fever pitch of anti-Manson sentiment.

Jump forward a couple of years and the perceived Columbine connection was still alive and well—flourishing, as a matter of fact. The mother of one of the Columbine victims traveled all the way to Scotland in August 2001 to advocate a boycott on Manson's performance at Glasgow's Gig on the Green festival. Citizens for Peace and Respect, a church group in the Denver area, decided in their infinite wisdom that the best way to promote said peace and respect would be to call for Marilyn Manson's performance as part of the Denver 2001 Ozzfest to be stricken from the free-wheeling concert conglomerate. Yup, that should do the trick. "We're against him because he promotes six things," the organization's founder, Jason Janz explained in May 7, 2001's *Rolling Stone*. "We believe he promotes hate, violence, death, suicide, drug use, and the attitudes and actions of the Columbine killers." Manson retorted with a quick one-two punch, deriding the religious group's use of the tragic school shooting as "a pitiful excuse for their own self-serving publicity," on his website, and declaring that in response to their protests he "will provide a show where I balance my songs with a wholesome Bible reading. This way, fans will not only hear my so-called 'violent' point of view, but we can also examine the virtues of wonderful 'Christian' stories of disease, murder, adultery, suicide, and child sacrifice. Now that seems like 'entertainment' to me."

Despite all of the terror and horror the world has witnessed since Marilyn Manson hit the (previously untainted) record store shelves, many religious groups and local governments worldwide continue to regard the artist as evil incarnate. Calls for cancellations of concerts continue to this day—in places as far-flung as Croatia and as close to the origins of the outcry in the good old heartlands of the USA. "I get criticized for being unpatriotic, but I believe that the most patriotic thing I can do right now is be an artist who pushes and tests to make sure that democracy's functioning properly. That's what we're fighting to represent as a band, that it's important to have freedom of expression and to make America a place worth fighting for," he told London's *The Independent* in its April 21, 2003 edition. The

irony in such widespread demonization of the man who declared himself the Antichrist Superstar to a relatively small legion of fans back in 1996 could be construed as sublimely poetic.

As for troubled teens, well, Manson had always been a dedicated champion of the disenfranchised. "A lot of what I say to our fans is 'Stop worrying about trying to fit into the status quo of what is beautiful and what is politically correct,'" he told *W* in its September 1, 2006 issue. "Believe in yourself and stick to what's right. If you want to be like me, then be like yourself."

As for Klebold and Harris—Manson's answer to why they did it? "Because they wanted someone to listen to them. And that's why they did what they did, because no one was listening. They didn't do it because of music or movies, they did it because they were angry," he told the *Daily Herald* in a June 8, 2001 interview. "And I have some anger, but I choose to express myself in music. And that's why art is important and special and worth fighting for, because art is where people can separate themselves from their darker side. You can release all your demons into what you create." As he succinctly and without hesitation answered Michael Moore in *Bowling for Columbine* when asked what he would say to the kids and the people in the Littleton community: "I wouldn't say a single word to them. I would listen to what they have to say, and that's what no one did."

DEATH VALLEY

Manson spent the most part of the end of the 1900s and the much-hyped transition into the brave new 2000s in seclusion, licking his wounds and creating what many took to be his artistic response to Columbine. During his self-imposed exile, he proclaimed that his website would be "my only contact with humanity."

Snippets of news filtered out of the Manson camp. Plans for a film, a novel, and a book of images in concurrence with the new album were all reported. The reclusive rock star announced the formation of his own record label at the end of 1999. Posthuman Records, founded in conjunction with EMI's Priority label, signed its first band in Washington, D.C.'s industrial goth outfit, Godhead. Although one's own label is the stuff of dreams for many musicians, Manson once again proved himself to be unconventional. After Priority Records had gone out of business and Posthuman Records was therefore defunct, Manson confessed in 2003 to *Outburn* magazine in its twenty-second issue that he found the experience "unsatisfying, because I don't like to try and manipulate somebody else's work into something that is marketable. For me, by nature, I create things that I think people will like, but it's part of my motivation and it's not money driven... It made me feel like the people I don't like in a lot of ways."

On November 14, 2000, *Holy Wood (In the Shadow of the Valley of Death)* was released. A far darker, angrier, more primeval work than its predecessor, *Holy Wood* most definitely belonged in Death Valley. The album was in part a study in the relationship between fame and death, with the likes of Kennedy, Christ, John Lennon, and assassins John Wilkes Booth and Lee Harvey Oswald popping up in the lyrics. Song titles such as "The Death Song," "Count to 6 and Die," and "A Place in the Dirt" signified Manson's mindset as he responded in kind to all of the negativity he'd endured in the wake of the Columbine tragedy. The lingering stench of Columbine was a conspicuous presence within the album's 19 circumspect songs. In the beautifully pared-down "Lamb of God" Manson quietly, ominously

growls, "*If you die when there's no one watching / Then your ratings drop and you're forgotten.*" The tribal beat of the album's first single, "Disposable Teens," is a fitting backdrop to the line "*I've got a face that's made for violence.*" And there was no doubting the inspiration of the haunting dirge that is "The Nobodies" (*We're the nobodies / We wanna be somebodies / When we're dead / They'll know just who we are.*)

Holy Wood managed to offend people before they even heard it, or indeed, managed to remove the shrink-wrapping. The culprit was the cover artwork, depicting a bloodied, jawless Manson in a crucifixion pose. US retailer Circuit City, "in the best interests of all of our customers," went to the lengths of covering all of the CDs in its over 600 stores with an "alternate" cardboard sleeve. Another big player in the chains, Best Buy, figured it would be safe to sell the CD with the original artwork as long as it opted for the less-scary version in all advertising. Manson posted his gleeful reaction to all of this on his website, writing, "The irony is that my point of the photo on the album was to show people that the crucifixion of Christ is, indeed, a violent image. My jaw is missing as a symbol of this very kind of censorship. This doesn't piss me off as much as it pleases me, because those offended by my album cover have successfully proven my point." Other retail giants such as Wal-Mart and Kmart simply refused to sell the album altogether, as Manson wasn't offering up an edited, cleaned-up version sans the parental advisory warning. The Catholic League came out in public condemnation of *Holy Wood*, advising good Catholics the world over to boycott the CD; as League President William Donahue—according to PR Newswire's November 30, 1999 report—declared, "This guy is at war with Christ."

The album was critically lauded but did not pack a huge commercial punch, racking up relatively low sales numbers. "*Holy Wood* won't win converts, but its creator's commitment to fighting back at a society hell-bent on martyring him makes the self-indulgence universal," read *Rolling*

Stone's review. "There's a little Manson in all of us. Or there should be." The *Washington Post* described the album as "a full-frontal assault on the senses" and proclaimed, "Manson's rage within the machine is palpable throughout *Holy Wood*, and disturbingly well articulated within its pounding pulses."

The album is the third piece in a cryptic triptych, tying itself in with *Antichrist Superstar* and *Mechanical Animals* to form a seemingly autobiographical threesome about "a boy who wants to become part of the world that he doesn't feel adequate for, and the bitterness and rage becomes a revolution inside him, and what happens is that the revolution becomes just another product" as Manson explained to *Rolling Stone* in its July 29, 2000, issue. "When he realizes it's too late," Manson concludes, "his only choice is to destroy the thing he has created, which is himself." An epic work conceived, arranged, and co-produced by Manson, this concept album showed ample evidence of the careful crafting that went into its creation.

The recording of the album was a fittingly dramatic experience. The band took over the former home of celebrated escape artist Harry Houdini. The house was rumored to be haunted, and the band found themselves able to attest to a host of inexplicable occurrences (such as pianos playing themselves at night). "We chose not to go into a studio and ended up taking over the Houdini mansion, which is where we set up and lived to do the album," Ginger Fish told *Drum!* in its January 2001 issue. "We brought in every piece of gear we could find, and lived around it, breathed it in, and just went from there. There were five studios set up in the house, so there was a creative flow moving in every room. The sound is amazing." The freedom so much space afforded the band had a profound effect on the music-making process. "It took a long time to do, but it was really cool," Pogo (who possesses a sky-high I.Q.) told *Kerrang!* in its November 2000 issue. "Most of the time, I went upstairs and worked on a computer and synthesizer. I messed around with prime number loops where they only

intersect every three days and I'd check up on what kind of music they'd be making. You never know what's going to happen." Twiggy told *Guitar World* in its January 2001 issue, "I remember when we recorded the bass for 'Cruci-Fiction.' The monitors weren't big enough to play in the control room, so we ordered these giant speakers. I think they were $30,000 each, or something like that. Someone rented them to us. I don't even know what they were called, but they were supposed to be impossible to destroy. They're supposed to be unblowable speakers. But we got the mix cranked up on them and they started blowing smoke rings. Actual rings of smoke came out."

The band took the 23rd Psalm "in the shadow of the valley of death" quote to heart, and spent time camping out in Death Valley during the making of the album. "We just went to the desert to explore," Twiggy told *Guitar World* in its January 2001 issue. "We brought some acoustic guitars and I brought a little Indian drone machine. We went out there just to write a few little things and maybe perform some of the songs out in Death Valley. The desert at nighttime is real scary. We made up a story that there's such a thing as desert bears. Which of course there isn't. We told John 5 that desert bears were going to get him."

"I think the battle with *Holy Wood*, I find it symbolically kind of ending with my statement in *Bowling for Columbine* and going back to Denver and playing there and not getting killed, which I think everyone pretty much expected. Even I was willing to take that risk," Manson asserted in 2003's *Outburn #22*. "That felt like I conquered something that I had started with *Antichrist Superstar*, and I saw it through and I showed people that I was a survivor."

Marilyn Manson emerged from its temporary cocoon with roaring, raging colors, celebrating the release of *Holy Wood* with a far-reaching five-month world tour brazenly entitled "Guns, God, and Government." The no-holds-barred traveling show realized the potential evident in the earliest Spooky Kids gigs. The distinctive brand of performance art

that Manson had since honed and toned within an inch of its life thrived in the large-scale arena setting in front of seething crowds.

Manson onstage is a sight to be seen. His fantastically theatrical wardrobe is made up of an inspired collection of ripped stockings, leather dresses, eight-inch platform boots, enormous bat wings, lederhosen, top hats, Mickey Mouse ears, a 50-foot-high mechanically-elevated skirt, military get-up, prosthetic limbs, stilts, crutches, corsets, a golden Pope robe (complete with clergymen's hat of choice, the papal mitre), elbow pads, knee pads, crash helmets, clothing fashioned out of the likes of road-kill and ostrich spines, thongs, and a giant strap-on cross made of TVs.

All of which is visually dramatic in and of itself, but Manson utilizes his costume as a custom-made tool to craft an otherworldly physical persona. His bare chest, lacerated with a spider web of pallid scars, emerges like a charmed snake from his black leather corset. Dissected into a black and white juxtaposition of clothing and the palest of flesh, his body jerks and twitches its way across the stage. The handicapped mutant that towers above the stage in stilts and extended crutches is utterly captivating as he maintains his precarious balance while painstakingly making his spider-like progression. Manson's stirring entrance aboard a gladiator's rickshaw pulled by two nearly nude women with horses heads is all the more effective for the giant headdress of black plumage he wears with regal pomp. A horse-tail epaulet is transformed into another limb as his frenetic arm pumping ensues.

A chaotic cornucopia of pyrotechnics, lighting, backdrops of smoldering American flags and crucified fetuses, burning crosses made of guns—these are a few of Manson's favorite things that make up the band's impressive stage set. The grand finale of the "Guns, God, and Government" tour was a concert at Los Angeles' Grand Olympic Theatre specially filmed for an In Demand Pay-Per-View special. The president of Eagle Vision, Steve Sterling, told PR Newswire

on August 7, "Working on this extraordinary project with Manson has been one of the most intense undertakings of my career. The program contains some of the most high-end production values we've had on one of our shows."

Further key ingredients to the audio-visual feast for the senses that is a Marilyn Manson concert are the other band members. As riveting as Manson is, he's got fierce competition. Twiggy's mile-long dreadlocks flail whip-like around his Medusa's head. The spikes of M.W. Gacy's mohawk reign over his desperate attempt to keep reins on either his keytar or his keyboard which is, astonishingly, attached to the stage by a giant spring. John 5, resplendent in a floor-length black thrashes his platinum locks into a sweaty frenzy as he punctuates his precision power playing with Pete Townshend-worthy jumps.

Manson is in perpetual motion onstage. He marches, crawls on his hands and knees, rolls on to and off of the risers, convulses, crouches, and throws himself around like a man battling an invisible foe. His long limbs extend in every direction, pointing, saluting, punching, pulsing. Impromptu stripteases are over in the flash of an eye. Lewd gestures, crotch grabbing (mainly, although not exclusively, his own), and simulated sexual acts are compulsory. Draping himself over Twiggy, running headlong into John 5 in the midst of a guitar solo, throwing himself into Ginger's drums – he is a human tornado. "Since the day I joined, it was like being in *Full Metal Jacket*," John 5 told MTV on April 6, 2004. "Being onstage with Marilyn Manson is like being in a war zone. You never know when he's gonna freak out and throw shit at you. I loved every minute of it." "The show, while being theatrical, is very much raw, and it's operating on chaos," Manson said in an October 27, 2000 interview with the Minneapolis *Star Tribune*. "So I like to create different elements in the show that have to be followed. But the rest of it, I don't tell anybody else about—even the band. Then it's just whatever happens, happens."

That age-old mantra, "Somebody's going to get hurt," is

proven true yet again—and again—on the Manson stage. Manson's attack on Ginger Fish's drum set at New York City's Hammerstein Ballroom left the drummer with a fractured collarbone, and prompted mellower musician Moby to tell the *New York Post*, "It was disgusting. I'm waiting to see if the police want witnesses. That kind of violence is totally unnecessary onstage." Which of course prompted Manson to retort, "On my stage that kind of violence is completely necessary, it's just unfortunate that Moby wasn't injured. My drummer has offered to beat him with his good arm, though," according to a December 1, 2000 PR Newswire report. In 2004, Ginger's fall from his drum riser during a concert in Germany landed him in a Cologne hospital with a laundry list of reported boo-boos including a broken wrist, a fractured skull, and a concussion. "I get injured every night just about," John 5 told *Guitarist* in its February 2004 issue. "Everyone in the band has had a pretty bad war injury. Our drummer got his collarbone broken and his head split open. Our keyboard player got his head split open. On the *Mechanical Animals* tour I got hit with a bottle and it knocked one of my back teeth out. I get knocked over all the time. I get slammed into so hard. When someone's gonna smash into you, you usually know a second before and you can tense your body up. But if you're playing and you're loose, you're gonna go flying." Chaotic, just the way Manson likes it—and to keep 'em guessing, no two shows are alike. "It's a lot of reading his mind and guessing," Ginger Fish revealed in a *Guitar Center* interview. "It's a mental thing on stage with Manson. There's not a lot of organization. Or rather it's really organized, but in a chaotic way... Like I said, I've been hit in the head, my set is trashed on a regular basis. They get wound up before a show and you just don't know what's going to happen. Every time I get onstage I'm saying in the back of my mind, 'This is the last show I'm going to be playing with these guys!'" Twiggy would later reflect in a June 29, 2005 *Kerrang!* interview, "Touring with Manson we were just on a fucking self-destructive rampage... destroying everything, destroying ourselves. The art-project side of things totally overtook my life."

Manson's set slashed and burned it way across the live music landscape, blowing away A-list bands at every turn. The legendary Manson performances at the MTV Awards are cited as highlights to this day. Manson killed at the UK's 2001 Reading/Leeds/Glasgow Weekend in Leeds, leaving big shots like Eminem, Green Day, PJ Harvey, Papa Roach, Queens of the Stone Age, Rancid, Staind, and The Strokes in the dust. The August 27, 2001 *Rolling Stone* review of the rock weekend declared that "the Eminem-lite performance was easily upstaged by Marilyn Manson," citing, among other strong stage moments, a "self-performed glow-stick enema" and summing up, "despite strong performances earlier in the day from the American-heavy lineup, Manson left a lasting sense of awe." In November 2003 The Birmingham *Evening Mail* raved, "The Bible shredding and self-mutilation incidents of past Marilyn Manson shows may be gone, but live, the shock is still one with the rock."

All stops weren't pulled out on the stage; the chaos continued backstage. No green M&Ms for this rock star—Manson's backstage request list allegedly includes one bald, toothless stripper for after-show entertainment for the crew. And let's not forget the legendary "enema parties" or the "dildo-cam." A never-seen film entitled *Groupie* that Manson originally wanted to release in conjunction with the "Dead to the World" tour has still to see the light of day. Manson confessed during a mansonusa.com interview, "My former manager suggested that it should be locked away in a safe never to be seen because it would ruin my career, and possibly put me in jail....I've had extremely close friends feel uncomfortable knowing me after seeing it, and only through the discussion of it were they able to come to terms with it. It goes farther than most people would ever go and it was genuinely intended to be something released at the time...I suppose I was probably just too unable to realize that my perception of what's normal was very different than other people's." What on earth the film has captured is food for thought, but Manson has also professed not to subscribe to the conventional rock 'n' roll approach to groupies; he told *Rolling Stone* in a June 12, 2003 interview, "Groupies are a

strange thing for me, because I have this fatherly Boy Scout-leader quality. I have a sense of respect for people who are a part of what I do, and I don't feel the need to disrespectfully abuse them." And Manson fans are nothing if not devoted. Shaving one's eyebrows is not sufficient homage-paying in the Manson world. Carving "Marilyn Manson" into your chest (and that's the girls), asking John 5 to spread a loved one's ashes on stage, bringing crutches to the show so that you're able to make your way home after removing and gifting your prosthetic leg to Manson – now that's more like it. That's real devotion. A peek behind the curtain was up for grabs, however, in *The Death Parade*, a short film included on the *Guns, God, and Government World Tour* DVD. The closest you'll get to the backstage world of Marilyn Manson, the film offers up plenty of classic lines like "I need painkillers and butterfly stitches," "Ozzy, do you mind if I have sex with your wife?" and "You're eating broken glass, what the fuck is wrong with you?"

Speaking of jail... regardless of what was going on back-

stage, what went on onstage was apparently too much for some authorities. Whether it was the sight of Manson's bare buttocks parading around or perhaps just the blasphemous pope outfit, Italian authorities were suitably outraged to sick some two dozen Roman police on the performer following his February 2001 concert at the Palaghiaccio in order to slap him with two counts of public indecency. On September 21, 2001, Manson was served up with a sexual misconduct charge (a high misdemeanor with a possible prison sentence of one year) in Oakland County, Michigan, along with a side-dish of an assault and battery charge stemming from a July incident at the Detroit Ozzfest stop during which Manson allegedly rubbed his crotch against a security guard's head (and, please, who among us hasn't done that?). These charges were eventually reduced to fine-carrying disorderly conducts after a judge heard three hours of testimony. This was not, however, the first time a brief affair between Manson's crotch and a security guard's head had ended up in court like a bad marriage. In September 2003 Manson was cleared in a civil lawsuit filed by a guard who was seeking in excess of $75,000 to help him get over an episode that took place during an October 2000 concert at the Orpheum Theater in Minneapolis. "The path to truth is obscured by frivolous lawsuits, but it's lit by the objectivity of a jury that sees the difference between entertainment and assault," Manson stated. "I feel completely vindicated, and I'd like to thank the jury and the judge for their thoughtful verdict." As he told *Q* magazine in its April 2004 issue, "I proved that it was total bullshit...some people saw an opportunity to sue somebody for doing something stupid. I was glad that the jury saw through that. And this jury had born-again Christians and older people in it, people that wouldn't normally take my side."

"The blame, I don't get tired of. It's become part of my personality. And I can't say I haven't asked for it right out of the gate, with a name like Marilyn Manson. But lawsuits and things like that are tiring, because people try to silence me as an artist," Manson commented in *Interview* magazine's October 1, 2002 issue. "I'm not going to take it sitting down. I'm not going to take it in the ass any more—unless I've brought the lubrication."

Whatever the reaction to the live spectacle of a Marilyn Manson performance, the very fact that the stage show provokes reaction—be it inspiration or outrage (or, ideally, both)—is precisely the point. Manson's campaign of shock and awe isn't meant to be easy to withstand. "Art is a question mark, and everybody wants it to be an answer. And that's why most of entertainment is boring," Manson declared in a July 3, 2003 interview with the Los Angeles *Daily News*. "I like to be the musical version of someone yelling 'fire' in a movie theater," he told the *Daily Herald* in a June 8, 2001 interview. "A lot of music you just go and see it and it's just like oatmeal, you neither hate it nor like it, it's just there," he told *What* magazine in its April 1, 1999 issue. "I want people to feel something." Amen to that.

SEXORSHIP

The next epoch for Manson & Co., which he baptized "The Golden Age of Grotesque," was to begin with the end of a nearly decade-long personal and professional relationship. Twiggy Ramirez and Marilyn Manson, intrinsically linked for so long, severed their ties. In May 2002 Manson put forth the statement, "Unfortunately, I feel that Marilyn Manson, as a lifestyle, is not where his heart is. So I have decided to let him go his own way, otherwise it wouldn't be fair to us, the music, or especially to the fans. Although you can never replace a best friend like Twiggy, this album and new lineup will redefine anyone's idea of what Marilyn Manson is capable of."

"If I had said something when the bomb dropped it would have been too emotional, so I chose to keep my mouth shut and not say anything I might have regretted," Twiggy told *Kerrang!* magazine in its December 3, 2002 issue. "But really there was no big drama. We just grew apart in different directions and we both decided we wanted to do different things. We were together for so many years without any waves, and something was bound to happen eventually. We had a pretty successful run." Twiggy went on to work with Queens of the Stone Age, A Perfect Circle, Goon Moon, Oasis, and, eventually, Nine Inch Nails. The irony of Twiggy becoming a member of NIN wasn't lost on him. "It's almost a way of reconnecting with my past and moving on all at the same time," he mused to *Kerrang!* on June 29, 2005.

"I think his relationship in the band became old to him," Manson reflected in the October 1, 2002 issue of *Interview* magazine. "It's like when you're married to somebody and you start sleeping with other people. It was a tough decision, but we decided it was best that he go somewhere else so he would have his interests fulfilled. Hopefully, some day I'll have my friend back."

The band began work in the studio without one of its main songwriters, but rather than mourning his loss they found new strength. "With no disrespect to Twiggy, [his departure] helped the record, because it freed us from a lot of things I felt tied down to," Manson told *Blender* in its May 2003 issue. "You have to understand that it's my vision, and the people in the band aren't agreeing because they're in the band; they're sharing the vision. People will say it won't be the same with this lineup. It's not meant to be the same. It's meant to be better."

Swedish-born Tim Skold (formerly of Shotgun Messiah and industrial outfit KMFDM) took Twiggy's place on bass and co-produced the album with Manson. "When Tim Skold joined us as a producer, he put in the same energy and enthusiasm I put in. Personally, I think he is one of the best producers I ever had the pleasure to work with," Manson raved in a May 2003 *NY Rock* interview. "In the past, we seemed to have the tendency to put too much on an album. It was almost an overload. On *The Golden Age of Grotesque*, we worked more detailed, so that every song expresses exactly what we want it to express. It's sometimes easier to focus on something if there isn't too much around it. Like a painting, if there is too much in the painting you get distracted a lot easier by the multitude of images instead of concentrating and focusing on what it's really trying to say and express." Manson, as always, maintained sole claim to the title of lyricist, but the new songwriting team of Manson, 5, Skold, and (on occasion) Gacy turned out a fresh, tight sound unlike any of the band's prior studio work. "[Skold] has turned out to be the guitar god Marilyn Manson always needed," he told MTV on October 28, 2005. "His guitar playing is something that completely seduced me into liking [music] again. It was almost a naked woman to a man who's just gotten out of prison, because I felt like I was in a prison of sorts, of my own creation."

"Understanding stream of consciousness is sometimes very pure and of a deeper intellect than something that's very carefully thought out. I found control by letting go on this record," Manson told MTV on May 13, 2003. Letting go indeed. Manson allegedly submitted recordings of himself talking to his cat when the record company asked to hear how the record was coming along. He himself has speculated that the not-particularly amused label execs were ready to pull the plug on the whole project and have him committed. During the making of the album he updated his fans via online journal entries on his website. A September 9, 2002 entry entitled, "Cross Your Fingers, Not Your Legs," advised, "The album is a catalogue of emergency room costume party break-your-nose dancing ritualistic cattle mutilation backyard burlesque whores d'oeuvres that will end in a pleasant family-restaurant dinner. Even dessert, since you kids got all 'A's."

The Golden Age of Grotesque debuted on May 13, 2003 at Number One on the U.S. charts, pushing gangster-rapper 50 Cent's Get Rich or Die Tryin' down to the Number Two spot. To see evil old Marilyn Manson reigning over a Top Ten comprised of the likes of Norah Jones' huge run-the-bath-and-light-some-candles hit Come Away with Me, American Idol Kelly Clarkson's Thankful, The Very Best of Cher, and the Lizzie McGuire Movie soundtrack was just too good. Steam must have been coming out of the religious right's wholesome ears.

Reviews were mixed, but the naysayers seemed more begrudging of the band's endurance than honestly unimpressed. Rolling Stone couldn't seem to make up its mind about the album, declaring that the song "This Is the New Shit" sounded "a whole lot like the old shit" but adding, "What's surprising is that there's still so much life in what Manson is rehashing." London's The Independent cited "the stagnant state of the band's quaking techno-rock, which hasn't broken new ground since last millennium," in its May 16, 2003 review. The May 2003 issue of Blender called the album a "thrillingly over-the-top piece of work." MTV declared it "sleazy and celebratory," "a golden achievement," and "wicked, nonconformist, and musically compelling."

The highly stylized video for "This Is the New Shit" unveiled Manson's newest incarnation. Whether sucking on a woman's fingers with his newly metal-encased mouth or intoning "Let us entertain you" onstage, he introduced a new age that definitely deserved its golden label. The hyper-hypnotic chant of "Babble babble bitch bitch / Rebel rebel party party / Sex sex sex and don't forget the 'violence'" served up the new shit on a silver platter—and devilishly delicious it was.

The album is debatably the most blatantly sexual offering in the Manson catalogue. Manson's voice is irresistibly seductive as it whispers, screams, and teases its way through the musical landscape, and sex permeates the lyrics. "Vodevil's" chorus is "Kiss baby kiss / Bang baby bang / Suck baby suck / It's Vodevil." In (s)AINT Manson roars, "I've got an F and a C and I got a K too / And the only thing missing is a bitch like yoU." The incantation "You are the church / I am the steeple / When we fuck / We're all god's people" closes "Slutgarden." The song "Para-Noir" features a montage of women's voices gleaned from an experimental session in which Manson elicited the comments of a few dozen strangers. "I wanted them to let out their deepest, darkest feelings on why they fuck people, whether that is metaphorically or literally," he told Outburn's 2003 issue #22. The "mOBSCENE" video showcases a chorus line of high-kicking bombshells replete with stockings, garter belts, and scarlet red panties, as well as a cameo courtesy of Manson's ultra-sexy striptease artist girlfriend, Dita Von Teese. Manson himself, decked out in beautifully tailored suits and lavish false eyelashes, is at his most gorgeous and chockfull of good old-fashioned sex appeal.

Manson's muses for The Golden Age of Grotesque were two eras that piqued his personal interest, namely the glamorous Hollywood of the Thirties and the Weimar Republic years in Germany between the first and second World Wars during which there was an explosion of modernism—in architecture, art, dance (burlesque and cabaret), literature, and film. Both intensely creative periods also bred more than their fair share of condemnation and censure. "I took a lot of my inspiration from the artists in the late Twenties in

Berlin and then all the people in Hollywood in the Thirties that were hammered with censorship and called degenerate," Manson explained during an appearance on *Late Night with David Letterman*. "I found a common bond with those artists because I've been persecuted so much myself."

Manson imparted an interesting theory during a December 1, 2000 interview on MTV. "All I can really say is that I think that art and especially music thrives under conservative rule," he opined. "I think that Bill Clinton's attempt to be friends with young people, to come on MTV, did something to the rebellion barometer. It didn't really give kids any authority to go against. I think that that's why there's been a lot of bland and happy-go-lucky music created over the past six or seven years. I don't really support Bush, but I hope we get some good, right-wing, Manson-hating people in office so that I can piss them off."

Manson elaborated on his attraction to the mores of 1920s Berlin and 1930s Hollywood in a July 3, 2003 interview with the Los Angeles *Daily News*, saying, "People had a different attitude about entertainment and art. People wanted to walk around and live like they were in a movie. And now, because reality is what people watch on TV with reality shows, it's doing the reverse, and it's just not exciting to me. I prefer to live in a fantasy world."

"In some strange way, this record is more uplifting, only in that it's kind of a desperate celebration of life in that there may not be a tomorrow," Manson reflects in *Outburn*'s issue #22. "It's a different type of nihilism for me. It's not about

me maturing; it's about me actually finding a true release from this fear of dying...it strangely expresses my personality in a way that I hadn't captured before. I feel like when you listen to it, it's like spending that time that the record is being played with me."

Berlin was the oh-so-appropriate opening date on the "Grotesque Burlesque" promotional tour, which also featured Manson's artwork and a taste of striptease action from Dita Von Teese, "The Queen of New Burlesque." Marilyn Manson then embarked on the "Against All Gods" 2004 – 2005 world tour, bringing its grotesque brand of performance art to the masses.

"I'm sick of people who think art has to be beautiful and pleasing to the eye," Manson told *NY Rock* in its May 2003 issue. "Art can be beautiful, but at the same time it can be scary, grotesque, and frightening...If you look "grotesque" up in the dictionary it means 'departing markedly from the natural, the expected, or the typical.' For me, that is simply another word for individualism."

TAINTED LOVE

Marilyn Manson managed to shock the conservatives yet again by subscribing to a very conventional tradition when he proposed to his long-time girlfriend and future wife Dita Von Teese to the tune of David Bowie's "Be My Wife" in March 2004 in their home in Los Angeles. Their fairy-tale wedding stopped short of taking place in a church—opting instead for an opulent Irish castle—but Manson entered into the state of matrimony nonetheless.

In fact, this wasn't the first time the concept of marriage had reared its head in Manson's life; he was previously engaged to actress Rose MacGowan. The couple's couple-dom was memorably broadcast loud and clear when Rose managed to upstage a flamboyantly garbed Manson on the red carpet of the 1998 MTV Video Music Awards in no more than a thong and a mesh "dress" which made Elizabeth Hurley's infamous Versace safety-pin number look like a snowsuit.

The subsequent Manson-MacGowan engagement inspired the March 1, 1999 issue of *Newsweek* to crow, "Parents of America, your daughters are safe." "I think it's an amazing thing to tell someone you want to spend every day for the rest of your life with them," MacGowan enthused to *Interview* magazine in its May 1, 1999 issue. "Right from the moment we've been engaged, I've felt that the invisible threads binding us together have become even tighter. It's very sweet, actually. I can imagine being with Manson at 65." Her imagination was apparently running away with her however, and on January 18, 2001 MacGowan released a statement announcing the couple's split which put forth the rather incriminating testimonial, "There is great love, but our lifestyle difference is, unfortunately, even greater." She elaborated a bit in the November 1, 2001 issue of *Details* magazine, stating, "I couldn't take his lifestyle. The drugs? More than you can imagine. I realized it wasn't a lifestyle I wanted to be married to. I have never been a rock chick."

Manson described his time with ex-fiancée MacGowan as "a really damaging relationship" in the March 2004 issue

of *i-D* magazine, adding, "I won't say anything against her, it's about where I was mentally. I felt bad about who I was; I was made to feel that nothing I could do would be good enough...I was really just killing myself slowly day by day." He revealed to Knight Rider/Tribune News Service on August 1, 2001, "I think we had a mutually destructive relationship. I don't think Rose understood that I was quite as troubled or obsessed as I really am. I think Rose thought that I was just a person with a really strong imagination who liked to create a character, but she found out that all those things I say and do are very much a part of my real life."

It was a sentiment Manson had expressed before: There is no separation between church and state here. Simply put, what you see is what you get. Marilyn Manson is not simply a static character he has created, but rather an ever-evolving reflection of who he is. Apparently, when the glare of the spotlight is snapped off and he is alone in his bedroom, Brian Warner does not emerge, Incredible-Hulk-style; Marilyn Manson is Marilyn Manson. "I think a lot of people don't take into consideration that I have feelings and they objectify me, they talk about me the way you would Mickey Mouse, for example. He's a creation, which in some ways I am, but the creation has no separation from the creator," he told the March 2004 issue of *i-D* magazine. After all, "I created him to have a personality because I didn't feel like I had one when I was younger," he explained in the April 21, 2003 edition of London's *The Independent*. "I don't bother to define what's reality and fiction when they work so perfectly together."

"People who get involved with me in any capacity need to realize I'm married to what I do. I can't be idle," he explained in the July 2003 issue of *Details* magazine. Words of wisdom that perhaps should have been heeded…

Along came a woman who seemed to be custom-made for a rock star with a strong allegiance for the bygone days of old Hollywood and a definite naughty streak: Dita Von Teese, the striptease artist credited for single-handedly bringing burlesque back. Curvaceous to a fault with porcelain skin and raven hair, the always impeccably turned-out bombshell had taken the art of dressing (and undressing) to all new heights. The femme fatale's trademark shows—in which she cavorts atop a life-size Swarovski crystal carousel horse and or bathes in a giant martini glass—are meticulously crafted, lavish extravaganzas the likes of which garner universally breathless rave reviews. Whether as lascivious headliner for three years running at the burlesque revival showcase Teasorama, co-performer with Carmen Elektra and the Pussycat Dolls, or guest star at Playboy Mansion events, Dita made a lasting impression, and word spread.

"I've always been very obsessed with the illusion or archetype of what women should look like. Marilyn Monroe and Betty Grable and Bettie Page and Greta Garbo," Manson mused in the July 2003 issue of *Details* magazine. "Seeing a girl who looks like she stepped out of one of those photographs was what really appealed to me."

"I was cautious. I approached the whole thing very carefully," Dita told London's *The Daily Mail* in its Halloween 2005 edition. "I wasn't really into the rock-star lifestyle thing. I certainly didn't think this was the man I was going to marry."

Von Teese's original incarnation was a natural blonde named Heather Sweet who hailed from a small town in Michigan. Classical training in ballet combined with a penchant for playing dress-up in vintage clothing and studying the classic films of the Forties formed her childhood. Working in a lingerie shop as a teenager, she became intrigued with what went on underneath the outfits of women of past eras; once she had purchased her first Victorian corset, she was well and truly hooked. Through scrupulous study of the art of burlesque, she created a unique act and stood out from the crowd while performing as go-go dancer suspended from the ceilings of LA clubs in a gilded cage. Her stage name was borne of a photo shoot with *Playboy* magazine in the early Nineties and was inspired by silent film star Dita Parlo.

Dita's star was well on the rise when she and Manson dove headlong into a serious relationship. Jean Paul Gaultier was the first designer of many to sit up and take notice, and began dressing Dita for events. She flaunted her 16-inch corseted waist on the cover of the December 2002 *Playboy*. Her act soon became a must for any self-respecting celebration in the UK and, eventually, worldwide. Jade Jagger requested her services for the London Fashion Week fete for British Crown Jewelers Garrard Diamonds in 2003. British society bible *Harpers & Queen* reported in its September 2004 issue, "Like a diva in the classic mould, she brought the house down—and her host to his knees. By the time the goddess of burlesque Dita Von Teese had stripped to just a thong and a large cocktail olive, Ceawlin Thynn, who was celebrating his thirtieth birthday with a colossal party at Longleat House, was down on one knee and begging her to marry him. She wouldn't be swayed....Dita announced languidly, 'Honey, I'm already spoken for.'" The real-life pinup worked her magic for the unofficial royalty of England at the 2006 "Full Length and Fabulous Ball" held pre-World Cup at David and Victoria Beckham's British country estate known as Beckingham Palace.

Jetting around the world to delight audiences at star-studded private parties and high-profile public gigs is hard, albeit glamorous, work, but Dita didn't stop there. She took the lucrative step to a cosmetics contract when she was signed alongside Lisa Marie Presley, Debbie Harry, and Eve as one of the faces of Mac Viva Glam VI. In March 2006, Regan Books published her hefty 272 hardcover book *Burlesque and the Art of the Teese*. And just to round out her résumé, Dita starred in the award-winning short film *The Death of Salvador Dali* as Dali's wife, Gala.

Dita's signature retro look graced the pages of major fashion magazines, and she was credited as a significant influence on the fashion world, declared a muse time and again. In fact, the Manson-Von Teese partnership seemed to elevate both stars to the realms of the fashion elite. The ever-visionary Vivienne Westwood embraced the pairing, using the couple in her 2006 campaign as runway and print models. "Wow, what a couple!" Yves Saint Laurent designer Stefano Pilati exclaimed in none other than *Vogue* magazine in its March 2006 issue. "She's stunningly beautiful with fantastic style—someone who gives personality to her clothes—while he really crosses the boundaries in terms of style. It's not classical dandyism—he goes much, much further."

"I adore the ritual of getting ready for an evening out— whether I'm on the red carpet or just going out for dinner.

I'm high maintenance, but I'm not reliant on a glam squad," Dita told London's *The Daily Mail* in its November 6, 2006 issue. Indeed, the star still colors her own hair, assembles all of her outfits, and does her own makeup. In direct contradiction to the rest of Hollywood, she has neither a pair of jeans nor a stylist. Dita commented on her fashion philosophy in the February 1, 2006 issue of *Interview*, saying, "I love glamour and artificial beauty. I love the idea of artifice and dressing up and makeup and hair. I can't stand wearing the same clothes all day. It makes me insane. I like to dress for the afternoon and for dinner," and "I love the exaggeration of feminine beauty. I also love the look of a dandy, though. Obviously—I just married one."

The couple shared a taste for the exotic and provocative at home as well as on their respective stages. Decorator's touches like baboon heads and a menagerie of other taxidermist's treats share prominent placement with the likes of halved human brains and a human skeleton with an antelope's head named Ernie. Lots of people beautify their homes with collectible antiques, and Manson and Dita were no different. Well, not really. "'Oh, one of the most ridiculous stories is that we kept a dead baby in a jar and it was actually our baby. That's completely absurd, quite disgusting and offensive," Dita told London's *The Daily Mail* in its Halloween 2005 edition. "The fact is we do have a baby in a jar, but it's an antique medical specimen."

Dita seemed to appreciate the dichotomy in Manson's personality. "In some ways, he is intelligent, articulate, and reasonable, and in other ways he is decadent and frivolous," she reasoned in the October 31, 2005 edition of London's *The Daily Mail*. "We have a lot of different interests, but we're kindred spirits," she told London's *The Mail on Sunday* in its March 12, 2006 edition. She was as dedicated to her art as her partner was to his. "If you dropped by our house you wouldn't find us wearing sweat pants, sitting in front of the TV eating cereal—that's not our life. Our life is a little bit what you'd imagine, but then our stage personas are not that far from who we are in real life. What we do is who we are," she

told the London *Evening Standard* in its May 13, 2005 issue.

"I've found a woman I can relate to," Manson told MTV on October 28, 2005. "That's something—and I don't even feel sappy saying it—that, if anyone has that, don't lose it, because it's probably the only thing that you can ever really find any satisfaction from."

The December 3, 2005 Manson-Von Teese wedding was a grand and glorious affair, set in a suitably dramatic setting: Castle Gurteen in Kilsheelan, County Tipperary, Ireland. (The official civil ceremony had taken place the week prior in their LA dining room at midnight underneath a portrait of Marlene Dietrich and a brace of stuffed peacocks.) The gothic castle, owned by German artist Gottfried Helnwein, who had become a good friend of the couple's, was exquisitely done up in thousands of crimson and black roses, ruby-hued Swarovski crystals, and black lace drapes. The Hogwart's-worthy banquet tables were elaborately set with black and deep red Waterford (all the better to sample blackberry and absinthe sorbet), custom Wedgwood featuring the couple's monogram, black Irish linen, and spectacular candelabra centerpieces festooned with a burgundy explosion of roses, grapes, and love-lies-bleeding. There was a distinct lack of creamy whites.

Some 60 guests, including, reportedly, Ozzy and Sharon Osbourne, Keanu Reeves, Lisa Marie Presley, Johnny Depp, Madonna and Guy Ritchie, and Nicolas Cage witnessed the rather intimate ceremony. The wedding, a first for the 36-year-old groom and 33-year-old bride, was as high style as its locale. Mrs. Manson was ravishing in a purple silk and grosgrain taffeta gown made for her by Vivienne Westwood, which she accessorized with a Mr. Pearl corset and a Stephen Jones hat. Mr. Manson complemented his new wife in a black silk taffeta tuxedo by John Galliano. The wedding weekend, in true Dita-style, was a veritable celebration of costume change. Post-ceremony the bride slipped out of her wedding gown and into a floor-length black velvet and silk concoction

given to her by Jean Paul Gautier to cut the cake with her groom. For after-dinner dancing to the strains of Max Raabe and his 12-piece orchestra—famous for recreating Twenties and Thirties German dance and film music—Dita donned a Christian Dior sheath. She chose a green satin Moschino gown for the reception dinner the previous evening, held in the Victorian conservatory of Kilshane House. And let's not forget to mention the seven pair of Christian Louboutins the shoe designer (one of the honored guests) custom-made for the festivities. It was all so fabulous that *Vogue* itself commemorated the event in a full-color glossy spread in its March 2006 issue entitled "The Bride Wore Purple." Style most definitely reigned supreme.

"I do have an old-fashioned sense of tradition—although it's not always what everyone might find conventional. If you're going to do something like getting married, it should have a sense of celebration to it. It should be grand—it doesn't have to be in tracksuits," Manson told the London *Mirror* on October 2, 2004. He went on to profess his desire to procreate, musing, "I do want lots of kids, too, but not any time soon. Ultimately, that's how you make yourself immortal—by passing down your ideas and values to your children." The couple was married by avant-garde filmmaker Alejandro Jodorowsky in a (you guessed it) non-denominational ceremony. The officiate, dressed in head-to-toe white, read the vows which included the very Mansonesque promise, "Forever you will respect who you really are."

The union lasted just over a year. Dita moved out of the couple's home in December 2006 and filed for divorce at the Los Angeles Superior Court citing irreconcilable differences. She did not request spousal support. The January 5, 2007 edition of the *New York Post* quoted a friend as saying, "He's not been responsive. She loved him so much, but he has too many demons. He can't even communicate with her at this point. She tried to tell him she was divorcing him, but she can't even get him on the phone. She moved out of the house and he hasn't even noticed. She really tried to make this work."

ART & ABSINTHE

Meanwhile, Manson's wanderings along the polymath's path of exploration into the creative arts were taking him to some mighty interesting places. While we'd all been mesmerized by the music, the never-idle provocateur was stealthily and steadily carving out alternate Marilyn Manson niches in the arts, this time focusing on his fascination with painting and film. Let us not forget that this is a man determined to live his art on a daily basis. In the same way one might recall ordering in pizza and watching a DVD, Manson is one to nonchalantly come out with comments like, "The other night I took an 80-year-old taxidermied monkey, set it on fire in the pool, and filmed, it from beneath with an underwater camera," as he told July 15, 2005's *Rolling Stone*. "It was beautiful, like the Titanic, the Hindenburg, and King Kong all mixed into one."

Other rock stars have been known to dabble in the visual arts—Ronnie Wood and Paul Stanley come to mind—but Manson had been painting since childhood and never intended to "go public" with or benefit financially from his non-musical art. What was a solely private venture, a personal retreat of sorts, spilled out in the form of portraits of friends—such as Andy Dick and Dave Navarro—which he proffered as gifts. Once people began urging him to show his works, Manson reconsidered the clandestine nature of his craft. "I learned to accept and appreciate the fact that any art that you create isn't complete until somebody else receives it," he reasoned in *Outburn #22*.

An exhibition of 50-some of Manson's watercolors was put on at the Contemporary Exhibitions gallery in Los Angeles in September 2002. Contemplating the showpiece of the collection of works, a painting of a handless child embracing a toy doll entitled "Hand of Glory," Manson expounded, "The hand is a symbol of power and it represents stealing innocence and imagination from children. If you break down the whole show, that's what it's about. Me as a modern-day Peter Pan, not wanting to grow up. There's a difference between being immature and being able to still think like a child." As he declared in the March 2004 issue of *i-D*, "The most genius ideas are in the minds of children and lunatics. I describe myself as somewhere in between."

In keeping with his tradition of embracing the dark and the light, Manson uses a children's Alice in Wonderland metal paint box and a 1920s mortician paint kit intended for use on corpses, not canvases. He has also professed to accidentally dipping his paintbrush into his always-handy glass of absinthe during creative sessions, and the green tinge of evidence makes an appearance on more than one of his works.

Absinthe is a fitting cocktail of choice for Manson. It, too, has been vilified, singled out as a hallucinogenic poison capable of inspiring murderous acts. It has also been lauded as a creative stimulus by an A-list roster of fine artists—Van Gogh, Manet, Toulouse-Lautrec, and Picasso were all devout imbibers—and its effects were also appreciated by the literary set. Ernest Hemingway enjoyed a tipple, as did Oscar Wilde, who wrote, "The first stage is like ordinary drinking, the second when you begin to see monstrous and cruel things, but if you can persevere you will enter in upon the third stage where you see things that you want to see, wonderful curious things." The drink was so fashionable in 19th century France that it earned its very own version of Happy Hour as 5pm in cabarets and cafes became known as *L'heure Verte* (The Green Hour), and it was popularly known as The Green Fairy or The Green Mistress. The liquor borne of wormwood, anise, and fennel has been declared psychoactive due to the chemical thujone, and remains illegal in the United States since being banned in 1915. Due to its high alcohol concentration, absinthe drinkers usually undergo a rather elegant preparation ritual involving ice-cold water, the occasional sugar cube, and ornate absinthe spoons. "With absinthe, you don't find yourself drunk where you can't function," Manson told London's *The Mirror* in its October 2, 2004 edition. "You either have incredible dreams—I often wake up and paint or write—or you don't sleep for three days."

The grand opening of Manson's very own Celebritarian Corporation Gallery of Fine Art in Los Angeles took place on Halloween 2006. The show featured portraits of the likes of Edgar Allen Poe, Jon-Benet Ramsey, and a nude Adolf Hitler. The space is an invitation- or appointment-only gallery, and the Celebritarian Corporation is a collective art movement that is the brainchild, naturally, of Manson himself.

"I find it even hard to not sound pretentious by using the word 'art' so fucking often in sentences, but I think it's important to get the point across and not be ashamed of something that was once respected and will once again be respected on the same level of politicians and scientists and other things of that nature," he expounded in an interview on mansonusa.com. "Art is about creation and people that create are the closest thing you'll find to religion in the world. Without that, we wouldn't have dreams and without dreams, we wouldn't exist."

Manson's long-held interest in film and filmmaking had also been evolving. He found himself acting, and, eventually, writing and directing. It is not surprising that Manson's unique brand of charisma, innate sense of drama, and almost preternatural skill as an entertainer would translate to the big screen. After all, here was a man who had invented an entirely new persona for himself—and then lived it, breathed it, and became it.

"It sounds rather pretentious sometimes, but it's easier for me to just call myself an artist—if I decide to do music or if I decide to do a film, it works," he reasoned in the November 30, 2006 issue of *Rolling Stone*. "I just want to uphold a level of integrity."

Of course the music of Marilyn Manson was no stranger to the movie business, having appeared on soundtracks consistently for years. The band's contributions include a cover version of the *M.A.S.H.* theme song "Suicide is Painless" for the *Book of Shadows: Blair Witch 2* soundtrack (released on

his own Posthuman Records), as well as songs on soundtracks for a laundry list of movies such as *Beat the Devil*, *Bowling for Columbine*, *Dead Man on Campus*, *Detroit Rock City*, *From Hell*, *House on Haunted Hill*, *House of Wax*, *Life as a House*, *The Matrix*, *Mean Machine*, *Natural Born Killers*, *Not Another Teen Movie*, *Nowhere*, *Party Monster*, Howard Stern's *Private Parts*, *Saw II*, *Serial Killing 4 Dummys*, *So Fucking What?*, *Spawn*, and *Valentine*.

Manson's acting debut was in a movie made by a filmmaker with a marked fondness for surrealism: David Lynch. His 1997 film *Lost Highway* boasted a diverse cast list which featured Patricia Arquette, Robert Blake, Henry Rollins, and Richard Pryor, as well as Marilyn Manson and Jeordie White as Porno Stars #1 and #2 (respectively).

Manson's next major film role came along in the form of a cameo in 1999's high school murder flick *Jawbreaker*, which happened to star his then-girlfriend Rose MacGowan. His twisted taste in film roles persevered as his role in the 2003 film *Party Monster* attested. The movie tells the true story of Michael Alig (played by Macaulay Culkin), a prominent figure in the New York City club and party scene in the Nineties whose televised confession to murdering his drug dealer and roommate Angel Melendez was considered a wacky publicity stunt...until the body washed up from the East River. Manson was cast as Christina, a transsexual.

Up next was Manson's deepest and darkest character yet—in a film the *Boston Globe* called "Vile Beyond Redemption." In the 2004 adaptation of J.T. Leroy's book, *The Heart Is Deceitful Above All Things*, Manson played the part of Jackson, "the man I had sex with when I was ten," as Leroy frankly put it in the March 2004 issue of *i-D* magazine. The film tells the sordid tale of a young mother who reclaims her son from foster care to take him along on the depraved, drug-and-prostitution-riddled ride that is her life, starring Asia Argento and Peter Fonda. "The deeper you go with Manson," Leroy continued, "the more you are confronted, and that is the journey

he invites you on. To be a little bit scared, to be willing to go to uncomfortable places you wouldn't normally go to, to see through eyes that are shaded in the abnormal. Who else could play a man that has sex with a child in such a heartbreaking portrayal that makes you want to weep for him as well?" The veracity of Leroy's supposedly-true-to-life story was challenged when it came to light that the young, reclusive male author was in fact one middle-aged woman named Laura Albert, but the film rose above the cries of "literary hoax" and stood on its own strengths.

Set for release in July 2007 is the supernatural horror flick *Rise: Blood Hunter*, starring Lucy Liu and featuring Manson as a bartender. But enough with playing human beings. Manson lent his distinctive baritone to the extraterrestrial Edgar in the PS2 and Xbox game *Area 51*. Also starring the voices of Powers Boothe and *X-Files* veteran David Duchovny, the game is set in the US government's top-secret, high-security military facility that has for years been speculation HQ for conspiracy-theorists and UFO enthusiasts. "The thing about *Area 51* that was interesting to me was that I'd be portraying an alien," Manson told *GameSpy*. "It seemed kind of natural...the creature and I share a lot of similar feelings, that similar kind of distaste for mankind in general. And it's a game for people who don't necessarily trust the government, don't trust everything they're told when they're taught things in school...that's something I can relate to. I've always felt like an alien."

Manson became completely immersed in his next motion picture venture, taking the creative reins in both hands with his writing and directorial debut: the horror film *Phantasmagoria: The Visions of Lewis Carroll*. To top it all off, he is also scoring the film. The protracted project, currently in production and filming, will see Manson play Carroll, the writer most famous for penning *Alice's Adventures in Wonderland*, and will star young model/actress Lily Cole as a doll-like Alice. *Phantasmagoria*, by the way, is the title of a Lewis Carroll book published, interestingly, in January 1869, 100 years to the week that Brian Warner was born.

As usual with a Manson undertaking, all sorts of snippets of information swirl around the vortex. Talk of a special camera never used before in film, rumors of the use of a magician to conjure up special effects, the possibility of long-time friend Johnny Depp making a cameo appearance, speculation about the inclusion of Roxy Music's "In Every Dream Home a Heartache" in an otherwise period score...conjecture fueled by the delayed release date flourishes. "I just want to be unconventional by being traditional. I think by being traditional, sometimes like a Hitchcock, it's almost modern, because people are so used to seeing special effects," Manson told NME on June 30, 2006.

Manson has labeled 2006 the darkest year of his life, a year in which he found himself virtually paralyzed with despair. "Halfway through last year I was in such a black hole of depression," he confessed in the March 8, 2007 issue of Rolling Stone. "I couldn't make anything, I couldn't do anything, I lost hope." The delving into the personality of Charles Godgson (Lewis Carroll was his pen name) during the writing of Phantasmagoria may have contributed to his despondent state of mind. "I think I've found behavior patterns in common with him in my own life," Manson said of Carroll in the September 1, 2006 issue of W magazine. "And I can understand the alter ego aspect: Something happens in your life to create a schism, and because you can't live out certain fantasies or ideas in one world, you become somebody else. It's all pretty crazy, and I'm sure it's making me schizophrenic." It seemed that Carroll, too, had a bit of the opposing extremes of Marilyn Manson in him. "He was very much a Jekyll and Hyde story, and the more I looked into it, the more [I realized] this was a ghost story, really. He was haunted by his own demons and had a split personality in a lot of ways," Manson told MTV on February 15, 2006. "I think I was able to relate to that and to want to put it on the screen."

However Manson chooses to express himself, it is ultimately a form of art. "Entertainment can be art if it's used in the right way. Unfortunately, we grew up with the idea that entertainment is some lesser form of art, less valuable, less sincere, less worthy of our attention. I don't agree with it at all," Manson told NY Rock in May 2003. "I think any art that is able to move people, that somebody else feels something while they experience it, then it is justified and worthy, no matter what label it has or from which genre it comes."

Manson found himself teetering on the edge of a personal precipice, and only through returning to music was he able to pull himself away from the edge. Although he thought his music-making days were well and truly over, he began to compose the day after Halloween 2006, returning to the studio to create what would ultimately become the forthcoming album Eat Me, Drink Me. "As many dark places as I've gone in my life and in my music, this past year...it's a real wonder that I'm alive," he confessed in Revolver's May 2007 issue. "I never wanted to make music again, but this was the only salvation I had going for me. So somehow I came out of that, and I came out of that by writing a song, and that song turned into a record."

Manson once again shared production credits with Tim Skold on the new album. The team's experimental approach was evident in its use of the likes of a bottle of painkillers and the bringing together of a dildo and a leather couch as percussion effects. Innovative as ever. One element of old that was not in the mix this time around was John 5, who was informed in early 2004 that he was no longer a member of the band. "John 5 is a great musician, and that might be the very heart of the problem for him being involved in Marilyn Manson. Not because everyone else isn't a great musician, but that's not our focus," Manson reflected during a mansonusa.com interview. "It's about the power, the emotion. There's just something wrong about punk rock 'n' roll music being precise. He's a very skilled, precise guitar player, but it's like a craftsman. Craftsmen make hammers.

We're the people that like to use them." In fact, Manson took pains to fuck with that very precision throughout 5's tenure with the band. His nightly onstage assaults on the guitar player seemed expressly designed to throw the man's music off track. While 5, half grinning and half grimacing, held on to his riffs for dear life, Manson got a running start before battering him with full-on body slams. If that didn't do the trick, he'd pull 5's trench coat up and simulate anal sex – *rough* anal sex – banging into him from behind. Still playing, still precise? The lead singer would grab 5's head and force it into his own crotch. Deliberately sabotaging your own show may seem counterintuitive, but if you think about it, it makes perfect sense. Manson didn't confine his campaign of messing with 5's head (so to speak) to the stage, either. During recording sessions he

has compelled 5 to play outside in the rain or covered in blankets, and deliberately screwed with a rare guitar solo by blindfolding 5, shoving a headset onto his head in order to pump the audio from porn videos into his ears, and provided him with a succession of untuned, unfamiliar guitars. Despite reports that the relationship was strained and ended rather abruptly, John 5 had nothing but good things to say about his experience with Marilyn Manson, and indeed about the man himself. "I've never played with anyone like him," he told MTV on April 6, 2004. "And even after everything, I think that guy is a genius. He's really incredible, and he's going to be around a long, long time."

Although 5 was a major songwriting contributor for some years, there is no doubt that the Marilyn Manson machine

will yet again thrive in its newest incarnation. "If I had to do a record review, I'd say it's got a cannibal, consumption, obsessive, violent-sex, romance angle—but with an upbeat swing to it," he told the May 2007 issue of *Revolver*. Hold on—cannibal? The phrase "eat me, drink me" brings to mind both *Alice in Wonderland* and the Eucharist, but Manson has also said that the album's title is partially inspired by the sordid story of Armin Meiwes, a German man who sautéed and then devoured the penis of a willing victim he had found (where else?) online.

Eat Me, Drink Me promises to offer up scintillating lyricism, if the song titles are anything to go by. An anthemic "If I Was Your Vampire," a Manson-style ballad in the form of "Just a Car Crash Away," "You, Me and the Devil Makes 3," and "The Red Carpet Grave," are slated to join the album's single "Heart-Shaped Glasses." One can only presume that his split with Dita has informed the album's lyrics, if the song title "Putting Holes in Happiness" is anything to go by. All in all, it promises to be a very personal work. As he revealed to *Rolling Stone* in its March 8, 2007 edition, "This is very earnest and uncalculated and raw, in the sense that I know I'm fucked up, and I'm really not ashamed of it." The rock bible's April 2, 2007 issue labels the album "a mirror reflection of Manson's inner turmoil," and quotes him as confessing, "I've never been willing to write about myself in this way, because I didn't want to deal with the reaction from people around me."

Reaction has never been lacking in the Manson world, and we can be certain that this iconic agent provocateur's re-entrance into the music scene will be as spectacular and chaotic as ever. "I've been laying dormant, but it's not going to be just a gradual sneaking back into society," Manson warned in May 2007's *Revolver*. "It's going to be a very large swarm of pestilence."